*To my [?]
who due
"trips" with on [?]
bikes. Enjoy the
adventure!
Love, Charlcie*

Millennium Road

CHARLCIE HOPKINS

Book cover and design by Julie Felton.

ISBN: 978-0-9846748-2-4

CONTENTS

MILLENNIUM ROAD

INTRODUCTION

In spite of lavish media attention, New Year's Eve 1999 turned out to be a dud. Those who expected *Something Big* to happen were sorely disappointed. Y2K alarmists who'd emptied store shelves of generators and canned goods in preparation for worldwide calamity were left with dusty boxes cluttering their basements and garages. The US economy was humming along like a well-tuned engine and the bull market on Wall Street was churning out millionaires with no end in sight. At the beginning of 2000, the American Dream was not only hale and hardy, it seemed on an indestructible pathway to prosperity for all.

A few know-it-alls insisted that 2000 was not *really* the beginning of the new millennium but rather the final year of the old one. Two thousand and one was actually the Millennium Year. But by the time December 31, 2000 rolled around, most people were tired of millennium hype. The commotion as 2001 dawned was all about who would be the next president of the United States. The national election had come and gone but whether George Bush or Al Gore had the winning votes remained unsettled. As Florida officials recounted ballots and dramatically scrutinized "hanging chads" the true Millennium Year slipped in with hardly a bleep on anyone's radar.

That January I was at a point in my life where I was finally getting used to my kids being grown, gone and living busy lives of their own. My husband was still clawing at the corporate ladder but with waning enthusiasm. I had started a new job in 1999 but it wasn't exactly a career. I'd eagerly looked forward to the freedom of an empty nest but now that I had it, I wasn't sure what to do. No longer did I see my life proceeding in an ordered direction. On a deep level I understood that I needed something new in my life, something to stir things up a bit and restore zest for daily living. I saw the New Millennium symbolically as an opportunity for renewal within myself as well as the world at large. I wanted to *Do Something*, although what that *Something* might be I hadn't a clue.

On the first day of January I wrote in my journal: New Day, New Week, New Year, New Decade, New Century, New Millennium—2001! Now what?

I wasn't thinking in terms of anything dramatic. Mostly I just wanted to get off the same old track that it seemed I'd been on forever. My desire for change and adventure was entirely inner-focused and fueled. I wanted to do something *for* only, *about* only and *as* only myself. So while the year 2000 quietly shifted from one millennium to the next, I made a very private determination to get off my butt and take one of those less traveled paths so highly touted by psychologists, adventurers, philosophers and poets.

To better understand my restlessness, I took what was for me the daunting step of making an appointment with a therapist. I didn't want to come across as just another someone going through the stereotypical midlife crisis. I wasn't even sure I believed in such things. All I knew was that I'd spent most of my life doing exactly what was expected and had recently realized that expectations had run out. Along the way I had questioned—but kept most of the questions to myself. I knew it would be difficult to reveal my most private self to a shrink no matter how much I wanted answers. As it turned out, though, Dr. M's skillful probing soon uncovered aspirations that had lain dormant for far too long.

I had finally come to a time when I needed to be me. Oh, I know how that sounds. I'm embarrassed to say it. Plenty of people experience similar jolts of realization in their lives. Why so? In my case, it was the usual reasons. I'd spent most of my life acting out proscribed roles: daughter, sister, girlfriend, wife, mother, etc.

Those are the roles that generally defined women (at least to my generation) so that it seemed we were forever viewed, as well as saw ourselves, in the context of others. I had reached a time when I wanted to live deliberately as myself, for myself, on my own terms, in my own surroundings, *me and only me*. Yet to actually do so seemed not only a huge challenge but also selfishly indulgent. That was the essence of what quickly emerged in therapy.

I'd only been to several sessions when Dr. M. mentioned a friend who after a divorce had spent the next year on a retreat from her life. She bought a fifth-wheel trailer and pulled it here and there, stopping for a while whenever and wherever the spirit moved her. "Mostly," Dr. M. laughed, "She telephoned from some little town in the middle of nowhere where she was stuck waiting for a part to be delivered so that something could be repaired." From the profound state of routine in which I existed, being stuck in an unknown place, no matter where, while being entirely free and on my own, seemed not boring but redolent with possibility.

I randomly opened a road atlas, closed my eyes and jabbed a finger. *Ah ha!*—Mound City, Iowa. Who ever heard of that? What would one find in Mound City, Iowa? Then I jabbed again and hit near Mission Ridge, South Dakota. *Jab, jab, jab, jab!* My finger landed in Arizona, Louisiana, Pennsylvania and Maine. Dr. M's anecdote about her friend had put exotic ideas of back-roads exploration into my head.

Although I'd once been an airline stewardess (pre "flight attendant" days), I'd actually seen little of my country. I worked for a regional carrier that hedge-hopped across the South. Nevertheless, I'd found such places as Hattiesburg, Mississippi and St. Simons, Georgia, interesting in their own ways. I had always found the off-the-beaten-path and unsung locales nearly as appealing as the great cities and landmarks. Perhaps that tells something about my delight in travel. I began to think about seeing my country again but this time to go far beyond the South, and I did not want to see it from 30,000 feet in the air. I wanted to travel close to the land through small towns and large cities, along borders and farmlands, over mountains and bridges, through forests and deserts, by rivers and seashores, down dirt roads and two-lane blacktops, and on the great interstate highways that grid America east, west, north and south. If I met new people along the way, then all the better. But I was mostly drawn to reconnecting with scattered friends and family who I hadn't seen in a while. Most of all I wanted to see new things and have new experiences, and I wanted to think and write about what I saw and did along the way. All this came to me in an epiphany triggered by imagination, reading books and that second-hand tale of my shrink's trailer-hauling friend.

Once the idea was ignited, time seemed short. There was so much to think about, so much to do! First came preparation and the beginning of preparation meant research. How would I travel? Road trip was definitely in my vocabulary. My initial idea was to set out in my Ford Explorer but that plan floundered when I considered details. Motels and restaurants would be expensive as well as boring and limiting. I immediately began banking every penny I could into what I called my "travel account." Finally, I decided a great way to go would be to rent a motorhome. When I looked into that, however, the cost for an extended rental was exorbitant. Then I searched the Internet for a good used RV to purchase but the task was daunting. I knew so little!

I began to study books on RV travel. While surfing the Internet, I lucked onto Joe and Vicki Kieva's web site and ordered all their how-to handbooks. That was my introduction to what I now know is a substantial amount of information on the subject. The Kievas' books were an excellent first exposure because they were simple, technically sound and informative in practical and often humorous ways. Did I mention inspiring? Perhaps the most helpful manual I studied was Kim and Sunny Baker's *The RVer's Bible*. I read too many books about purchasing, maintaining, equipping and driving an RV to list them all. A pattern began to emerge in these books, many authored by people who had forsaken "normal life" for perpetual travel. Unbounded enthusiasm for life on the road permeated even the most technical texts and that is something I found especially appealing. I began to realize that my mental image of RVers as retired snowbirds was only a small piece of reality. I began to understand that a whole subculture of "on the road" enthusiasts wander the American continent as RV nomads.

The most important fact I learned from reading was that if you can drive and maintain a car, you can drive and maintain a motorhome. Yes, it's different but once you understand the basics, it's a snap. One day I hardly knew anything about recreational vehicles, in fact I disdained them as gas-guzzlers clogging up the highways. Within several months, however, I became an aficionado and would-be fellow traveler. As with almost everything, it took actually doing it to attain real competence. The nuts-and-bolts of RV'ing is not what this book is about. This is a story about why I did it, where I went, what I did, what I saw and who I met. In other words, this is about exploration and discovery both within and without. That, of course, is the essence of all good travel writing. A motorhome was simply the vessel that enabled my physical journey to progress as my mental and spiritual journey also made way.

The seed idea was planted in January 2001. After four months of reading books, researching Internet sites and visiting dealerships, my husband and I purchased a new 22-foot Four Winds 5000 motorhome. As motorhomes go, it was small. In fact, it was pretty basic but that's all I wanted. It came with a Chevrolet 5.7 liter truck engine that drove like...well, like a truck. It got between 10 and 15 miles to the gallon depending upon travel conditions.

Among other conveniences, my snazzy little RV was equipped with a stove, refrigerator, microwave, forced air furnace, air conditioner, generator, three water tanks, booth-style dining table (which made into a bed), sofa (that also quickly unfolded into a bed), television, toilet, two sinks, shower, and enough storage space if you didn't over-pack. There was also an over-the-cab queen-sized sleep area with super-comfortable mattress and overhead skylight. Company literature claimed the Four Winds would comfortably sleep six, but three or four would be more truthful. For two, it was extremely adequate. For one, luxurious.

The next several months I had fun equipping and getting used to driving the Four Winds. First, Jim and I took a shakedown cruise to the North Carolina Mountains, then a maiden voyage to the coast of Alabama. In between were many weekend jaunts—lots of learning experiences. By the end of August 2001, she was finally equipped and ready to hit the road for an extended journey. I'd given a month's notice of leave at work and although I joked that I might not have a job when I returned, my boss reassured me that I would. As final preparation, I reread Jack Kerouac's *On The Road*.

Of course, few endeavors run without a hitch. One week before departure my husband was summarily given "early retirement" from his company. This, of course, was just another euphemism for "you no longer have a job." It was a shock. Jim was still under sixty and not ready or prepared to retire. He suddenly faced looking for another job.

The summer of 2001 fuel was selling in South Carolina for the highest price per gallon anyone could remember and yet we were the second cheapest state in the nation for gasoline. It was all the way up to nearly a dollar a gallon. Then my boss decided he wasn't so pleased with my decision to disappear for three months after all. My determination was shaken. But Jim remained incredibly supportive and insisted that I do what I had to do. I really believe he understood. Fact is he was probably looking forward to a little respite away from me as well. Anyway, he seemed to understand that by then I was beyond changing my mind. The trip had taken on an almost epic importance in my mind and life plans.

All I knew was that I had to do it and I had to do it alone. Something drove me. A challenge? Of course. Vacation? That didn't explain it. Sabbatical? Yes, but more. I craved new experiences removed from the predictability and routine of everything familiar. The great travel writer Paul Theroux calls such feeling "the importance of elsewhere." I wanted to go new places and see new things, but what I needed perhaps even more was to explore within and test myself. I was overflowing with energy and longing for the experience and adventure I felt that I'd missed by marrying at an early age and almost immediately having two children.

Hasn't everyone wanted to get in a lovely vehicle and just hit the road? To follow the highway wherever it leads? From the many comments I received from friends and strangers alike, I knew my idea was hardly unique. The difference was that I actually did it. That's what this book is about—so that readers can vicariously ride along and share the experience.

So it was that on Sunday, August 26, 2001, a bright, hot and muggy day, I released the parking brake and drove quietly away from Rainbow RV Park in Taylors, South Carolina. No long farewells or fanfare, not even anyone there to see me off. Jim was playing golf. Many of my friends didn't know that I was leaving. It was just me and the Four Winds, neophyte voyagers, destination ...*America.*

Little did I know how profoundly the events of the next three months would change nearly everything.

CHAPTER 1

THE LEARNING CURVE

After months of preparation the day of departure finally arrived. I had mixed feelings for many reasons; eagerness and excitement intermingled with uncertainty and even anxiety. It was hard to fully grasp that the day had come for just me, the RV and the highway. I had vague notions of where I was going but nothing definitive. I'd purposely kept plans loose, wanting only to live in the moment, a modern-day wanderer. No more dreaming and scheming, no more thinking and planning; and no explanations. Just turn the ignition key, start the engine, and follow the road....

Jim and I met our friends Lynn and Bill for breakfast at Gene's Restaurant as we usually did on Sunday mornings before the guys headed to the golf course. Lynn surprised me with a bag of freshly baked blueberry muffins. She'd enclosed a bon voyage card that quoted Henry Van Dyke: *Those who would see wonderful things must often be ready to travel alone.* I thought, How apt! Before leaving I taped the card to a central spot on the RV's bulkhead next to the back door. I often read that card on my trip and it never lost its relevance.

Rosa, another friend who I hadn't seen for a while, also came into Gene's, and her unbridled enthusiasm for my "adventure" (which she hadn't previously known about) was encouraging. I'd shared my plans with only a few people so I was glad to see Rosa and tell her in person. If anyone wondered why I'd disappeared, I figured Rosa would pass the word around.

After breakfast, Jim dropped me off at Rainbow RV Park and rushed away to his tee time. No awkward good-byes and that's the way we wanted it. I spent another hour tinkering with last minute preparations and then, inauspiciously, got behind the steering wheel, took a deep breath and cranked the engine. *Voila!* I was on my way! When I reached Hwy 25 north, I turned the radio to a classical station and all of a sudden Strauss's Radetsky March was blaring from the speakers. I smiled to myself—it was a worthy musical flourish for what I hoped to be a great adventure. Hearing that dramatic march with such perfect symbolic timing seemed a good omen.

I drove first to Asheville, a beautiful mountain town about 50 miles north of my house. Near the Swannanoa River, I pulled off the road and called my friend Marjorie on my cell phone. Marjorie insisted that I wait right where I was until she came down from the mountain for a proper good-bye. How about lunch? Well, sure...although I wasn't the least bit hungry. She arrived 20 minutes later with gifts, several books on tape (pure escapist mysteries), the new Lucinda Williams CD and Woody Guthrie's *This Land is Your Land*. Earlier in the week my friend Julie had also given me a selection of *bon voyage* tapes that she'd carefully selected and copied from her own collection, songs about leaving, traveling, seeking new directions and hitting the road, etc. My idea was to begin my trip with as little fuss as possible but the thoughtful and unexpected gifts from friends were still much appreciated. Knowing they were supportive of my journey provided gratifying reassurance. I'd also heard from others who wondered why in the world I would want to take off to unknown places all by myself. What about my husband? What about my responsibilities? They just didn't get it. "If you're afraid of loneliness, don't travel," advises Theroux.

I followed Marjorie to a mall parking lot where I parked the RV, and then she drove us to downtown Asheville. I felt a little antsy because I'd put only 60 miles on the odometer and was already stopping. I wasn't yet comfortable with ignoring time. Shouldn't I be many more miles down the road by now? But then I realized *who cares? Who's counting? What's the hurry?* The realization that I had only me to consider began to sink in. It was simple but profound. I could do any damn thing I pleased! It was exhilarating to say the least.

Marjorie and I ambled along streets that were bustling with activity. On a warm weekend afternoon, the outdoor tables in front of restaurants were filled with people eating, drinking and talking with friends. People wandered in and out of stores and galleries. Marjorie steered me to a cafe on Biltmore Avenue and we sat at a window table. We ordered iced tea and the sampler hors d'oeuvres platter and chatted as we watched people stroll by.

It was difficult for me to sit in one place and relax. My mind was racing; I couldn't shake the feeling that I needed to be on my way. "You need to decompress after all the pressure of getting ready," Marjorie insisted, and of course, she was right. After several hours she drove me back to the mall parking lot and then suddenly I was in the RV again, once more behind the steering wheel and back on the highway.

Where to now? I thought about the many people who had told me how brave they thought I was...when my inner voice insisted I was only being self indulgent. Finally, I was alone in the motorhome, no need to consult with anyone but myself. It was an idea I was still working on but oh, so exhilarating. I decided that since there was no hurry I'd stop at the first RV Park I came to and as if in answer to my thoughts, a sign appeared just ahead. I pulled into a beautiful mountain park and was directed to a lovely spot on the side of a hill. It took me a long time to get hooked up and set for the night, making sure to check my list at every step. A pop-up camper was parked next door and I was surprised to see that it was inhabited by two youngish women. I spoke briefly with them but was too shy to introduce myself and get their story. It would take me several more weeks to understand that was what I should have done; it was the way of veteran RVers.

Next morning I woke to soft rain. I made coffee and puttered around waiting for the sun to come out. By eleven and no change in the weather, I decided it was time I learned to break camp with my rain gear on. It took twice as long and I was drenched by the time I got back inside and changed into dry clothes. But finally I was ready to roll again.

I backtracked and got onto the Blue Ridge Parkway before heading further north. Emotional decompression was finally happening. Sprinkling rain continued to blur the windshield and I missed much of the passing scenery because of the misty haze. I had no idea where I was going but after hours of winding along the rainy Parkway, I decided to exit and begin looking for somewhere to spend the night. The only place I could find was a tiny park near Glade Valley, unsure exactly what state I was in. The little park was shabby and unpromising but by that time I had little choice. After settling in, I decided my spot was actually quite charming. Deep woods hugged the Four Winds on two sides and gentle rain in the trees and on the roof created perfect relaxation music.

After hooking connections to water and electricity in the drizzle, I stretched out on my couch to read. Marjorie had loaned me a big, hefty book, Margaret Atwood's *The Blind Assassin*. It was the kind of book that would take a while to get through, a long, slow read, and that seemed perfectly suited to the occasion. It was no time for a page-turner. I was finally getting acclimated to a carefree attitude.

The next morning I slept late and woke feeling rested and full of energy. The rain continued but I broke camp anyway and soon found my way back to the Blue Ridge Parkway. I continued to drive in mist and fog deep into Virginia, passing few other vehicles. The only problem was that my cell phone wouldn't work in the mountains. But I didn't care. I was learning fast that being "disconnected" was okay.

My mood was light and easy until jangled by several events. First, I left the Parkway to go into a small town to find food. When I drove up a driveway to McDonald's, I bumped the steps under the back door. In my haste to de-camp in the rain, I'd forgotten to fold the steps back to where they fit snugly under the chassis. They were bent so badly that I couldn't pull them down again. Then when I stopped for gas at New Market, Virginia, I left my gas cap behind at the station. Jim had attached a piece of Velcro beside the tank to attach the gas cap while filling, but the wet Velcro wouldn't work. I sat the gas cap on the concrete and that was the end of that. I knew from then on I'd have to be careful not to let the gas cap out of my hand. At least no one else had to know how stupid I felt for forgetting to replace it—or for not properly re-folding the steps. Each mistake quickly became a learning experience.

I returned to the Blue Ridge Parkway and although it was still beautiful, I was unable to see clearly due to the rain and fog. However, there was something especially lovely about seeing the woods, mountains and valleys shrouded in mist. I continued to drive with no destination in mind, having no idea where I'd stay the night. With dusk I realized how tired I was and decided to seek a more populated area. I'd been driving randomly for a while when I spotted a Truck Plaza and pulled in among the 18-wheelers. I'd read that RV's were welcome to overnight at truck stops, so I decided to give it a try.

I soon realized I hadn't made the best decision. Instead of softly dripping rain and rustling pine needles, I was serenaded all night by grating gears and the steady rumble of diesel generators. Bright lights glared overhead and shined into my skylight. People walked around talking and making noise what seemed like all night. Once I peeked through the shades to see who was making such a ruckus and spied what may have been two hookers standing on the running board of the truck next to me, knocking on the window and cursing at the top of their lungs. It was 2:10 AM.

After my night at the truck stop, I decided to make reservations for the next night's stay. I carefully perused my campground directory and finally settled upon a highly advertised park to book for that night. The ad promised a lovely family friendly atmosphere with level asphalt "pull-throughs" and spotless accommodations. Perfect! When I got there, however, I found it not exactly as claimed. The "family friendly" apparently meant hokey plastic cartoon character decorations, a closed swimming pool and a price that was about $20 more than average. Plus, it was only about 50 yards off a busy highway. I had driven seven miles off I-81 in an attempt to escape road noise, only to find myself parked just off another noisy road. Amenities were minimal, too. I had to remove my water filter because the connection was so close to the ground it wouldn't accommodate the filter.

I decided maybe it wasn't better to make reservations ahead but to check a camp out in person before staying. At least I had finally learned that it was best to start looking early enough in the day to find a good place to stay. There didn't seem to be a problem with overcrowding. I figured that through dumb luck I had probably set out at the best possible travel time of year when kids were back in school and snowbirds weren't yet migrating.

A major lesson had been duly learned. Don't drive too many miles in one day unless necessary. For one thing, you don't see as much—and that is one of the main pleasures of a road trip. Also, too much driving meant getting to camp tired and yet with the hook-up process still to accomplish (no matter the weather conditions or how much daylight was left). Then it was time to fix or find something to eat. On days that I drove too far, I ended up exhausted, hungry and irritable. During that first week, I learned my lessons well. From then on I determined to maintain an unhurried and easy pace.

Still stewing about the tacky and noisy RV Park I'd gone out of my way to locate, I retrieved my friend Jeanne's email from several weeks earlier and realized that she might be leaving for vacation that week. I'd hoped to visit her and suddenly it looked unlikely. I called and she wasn't home but I left a message. It was one more example of bad planning on my part but I was learning fast!

CHAPTER 2

GETTING USED TO THINGS

I was still having a hit-or-miss time in establishing routine. I'd assumed there would be more free time for all kinds of things, especially writing. Instead, I learned it was necessary to get somewhere early enough to hook up, get settled, prepare and eat a decent meal—and maybe even take a short hike to undo the sedentary time spent driving. Nothing quite as tiring as sitting on your butt for six or eight straight hours. Only then did I have the energy and inclination to turn on the computer and write. As it was, I was still in figuring-things-out mode, and therefore a bit unsure of myself. One person doing all the chores took longer than I'd figured. Every day, though, I got a little quicker at it. And although occasionally frustrated, each day felt easier. I was certain that I was doing exactly what I should be doing and I loved every minute of it.

My morning at the tacky, overpriced—and *reserved*—park began unpleasantly. All night I listened to cars and trucks rumbling by on the nearby freeway. What a racket they made; it was worse than the truck stop. I slept fitfully. Then I awoke parked on a sterile slab of concrete jammed up next to a huge behemoth of a custom-painted diesel-pusher bus. I was in a beautiful area, the Shenandoah Valley, but there was nothing beautiful to look at near my concrete campsite with its silly plastic decor.

The first order of business was to replace my lost gas cap. I'd covered the tank with an aluminum foil make-do job. I got directions to the nearest auto parts store and headed back that way. Since I'd seen plenty of freeway, I decided to travel only on back roads. Did I get lost? I sure did and was glad of it!

I found myself driving through wooded rolling terrain sometimes interspersed with farms. There were fences crisscrossing grassy meadows and occasionally in the distance a stately home. At some of the farms sleek horses—thoroughbreds, I think—grazed and galloped. I saw an elegant group of riders trotting along decked out in equestrian gear.

Because I really wasn't sure where I was, I finally pulled off the two lane road and parked beside a beautiful small Lutheran church. I figured I was probably in Lebanon Church, Virginia. It was a tiny crossroads with some historical looking houses and the church. As I sat there examining my map, a black woman appeared carrying a bundle on her head. I couldn't believe it—she looked like something out of Africa. She wore a colorful skirt and walked with graceful posture, perfectly balancing the package on her head. She gave me a slight nod without tipping the load. I watched her till she strode out of sight.

Then ten bluebirds swooped down and perched on a bush about 15 feet from where I sat inside the RV with my window open. I know it was ten because I counted them. They ignored my presence. I tried to be very still; I'd never seen so many bluebirds together in one spot. The sun was brilliant and they looked iridescent with rust colored breasts. Either they were all males or the females weren't of a duller hue. I felt as if I'd somehow stepped into another realm. The elegant horses and houses, the lovely little wooden church, the woman with the bundle on her head and then the bluebirds! Such simple things to see and experience but that made me take a deep breath and say to myself, *Wow!*

After purchasing a new gas cap in Winchester, I got back on I-81 and followed it north through West Virginia and Maryland, then finally turned east onto state Hwy 30 at Chambersburg, Pennsylvania. My destination was Gettysburg. Almost as soon as I left the interstate, I looked to my left and there was a farmhouse with a huge Confederate flag displayed in front. I did a double take and wondered if I'd somehow taken a wrong turn and gone back south. But no, there it was, a flamboyant rebel flag flapping in the front yard of the first house I saw in Pennsylvania.

The slow drive to Gettysburg was welcome after the speed and traffic of I-81. I quickly found a good place to stay, the Gettysburg Kampground of America. KOA's cost a little more than I generally liked to pay but they could always be relied upon for good amenities, security and cleanliness. Best of all, I was given my own wooded, private cove. The woman at the desk directed me to the nearest grocery, Kennie's in downtown Gettysburg, where I bought a chicken and fresh vegetables. Once back at the campsite, I hooked up to clean water, electricity and cable TV. Then I prepared my veggies and chicken and set them to simmer in my Vesco slow cooker. Since beginning my trip, meals had been too often fast food or make-do and I was ready for some good hearty home cooking.

I sat a folding chaise outside in the shade and got my book out. The weather was delightful, yummy aromas wafted from the open window and there were still three or four hours of daylight left. I read for a while, then made phone calls and wrote postcards.

I had promised my daughter Leslie that I'd send her "tacky postcards" from each place I visited. I found a great one at the Gettysburg KOA with a rebel flag on the front that said, "Confederate Greetings from Gettysburg!" When I told my friend Julie about the postcards to Leslie, she asked me to send some to her, also. Then I decided it would be fun to have my own collection, so every time I bought postcards for others, I got one for myself as well and began taping them on the bulkhead beside the backdoor along with other souvenirs.

I had a lovely, sound sleep that night—nine hours! And I awoke to a message left on my cell phone from Jeanne. She said that her Caribbean trip wasn't for another month and she was home awaiting my visit. I called her and arranged to be there in several days. Then I settled back and continued to enjoy the tranquility of Gettysburg. I loved the quiet, secluded cove I had at the camp and was in no hurry to be on the move. Each day I took a long walk around the park, which was wooded but with a feeling of security. Then I showered in the very clean showers provided, and tidied the RV. My camp didn't have a sewage hookup but that wasn't a problem. There was a disposal facility at the main entrance and I found it more convenient to use theirs upon leaving than to hook up at campsite. I decided using camp facilities was the preferable way to go, better to use their hoses and not have to clean and re-stow my own. From then on I chose no full hookups unless staying longer than a few days.

From Gettysburg I remained on Route 30 through rural countryside and several small Pennsylvania towns. I also passed through the larger cities of York and Lancaster. I had already decided never to take bypasses but to stay on the roads that went through city centers so that I could see what each town looked like.

East of Lancaster I began to see Amish farms off the highway. Just beyond the tiny town of Gap, I stopped for lunch at a Burger King. After I ordered, the manager looked at me quizzically and suddenly blurted, "Are you Amish?" My mouth must have dropped open in surprise. After all, I was wearing khaki shorts, a tee shirt and tennis shoes. Granted, I had on no makeup but still...! "Well, no," I answered. Then he smiled, "Oh, you must be Southern! Sorry!"

I was bewildered that a man who apparently lived in Amish country would mistake me in my casual clothing for being Amish. It didn't make sense. I continued wondering as I drove slowly along, nibbling French fries and peering closely at the farmsteads visible from the two-lane road. Suddenly a black fiber-glass horse-drawn buggy clip-clopped out from a side street, pulling right in front of the RV. The buggy's occupants ignored me completely, as if they were purposely not looking—they owned the road. I had to hit the brakes hard and my diet coke sloshed onto the floorboard. The bearded man at the reigns wore a wide brimmed hat and plain black suit. His wife wore a white bonnet and long black dress with short cape, unadorned and elegant. Her hands were folded in her lap and neither one of them, both sitting very stiffly, gave me the slightest notice. Wisps of blond hair showed from beneath the woman's cap. I thought, *wow, she looks a lot like me!* It was true. We had similar features—she could have been my sister.

Was that why the Burger King Manager had mistaken me for Amish? Did the Amish have a "certain look"? Or do the Amish have accents similar to a Southern accent? It was a strange thing to happen and I never did come up with an answer. I was completely baffled but not unpleased.

The Amish farms were fastidious. The fields were meticulously plotted into mostly rectangular corn fields. The stalks were tall, lush and ear-laden; other fields had already been harvested. The huge barns were painted a deep red or gray and the two or three storied houses were white, light gray or tan. Each farm had one or more silos and other outbuildings, and everything looked perfectly maintained. There was nothing messy near the Amish farms. There was no equipment, debris, or clutter visible anywhere.

On the other hand, all around these pristine farms was a jumble of normal, unkempt civilization. Right outside the fence of one beautiful farm was a grease-splattered service station and on the other side a grubby upholstery shop. I noticed a used car lot, plastic pennants flapping on wires, smack against an Amish cornfield. Such extreme juxtaposition had a jarring effect.

It was late afternoon when I arrived at Jeanne's house in Chester Springs. The area was quite rural but also a distant suburb of Philadelphia. I was driving slowly along looking for her address when a minivan in front of me suddenly pulled over and stopped. A woman got out and waved me over. "You look like you're lost. Can I help you find something?" I told her Jeanne's name and she gave me directions. A very friendly woman!

The driveway leading up the hill to Jeanne's was long in length and lined on both sides with mature trees. The branches formed a canopy that brushed against the RV's roof. Jeanne wasn't yet home but had left a note that she had to work until eight or nine that night. Her job as an emergency room physician at the Chester Springs Hospital required long hours. There was a nice place for me to park in a shaded area about 75 feet from the house. The weather was clear and 68 degrees with a slight breeze, so I opened all the windows and set up my computer at the booth table desk. Working on a novel had been one of the aspirations for my trip but until that afternoon I'd written only in my journal. No more excuses! Finally I had a block of time to begin the writing I'd been putting off.

Jeanne arrived home about 8:30 and we had a great time catching up with each other's lives. I had met Jeanne several years previously when we both participated in an online LPGA golf fantasy league. At first I knew nothing about her other than she was a golf fan and had a great sense of humor. We finally met in person at the LPGA Championship Tournament in Wilmington in 1998. Many people had cautioned that it was crazy to meet someone in person who you really know nothing about, someone you—*horrors!—met on the Internet!*—but I was glad I hadn't listened to those people. Jeanne had become a good friend.

I enjoyed my short stay at Jeanne's house. The one thing a little less than perfect may have been the food—not that I complained. Jean had been a vegan for many years and it was my first experience with soy burgers. But hey, I wasn't at Jeanne's house for the cuisine. Just being in that lovely place with a good friend was a huge treat!

Jeanne's house sat at the crest of a hill on 40-something acres overlooking distant mountains. It was near Chadd's Ford where the great American family of artists, the Wyeths, lived and painted. It was a very artsy area—off Art School Road—and also just a stone's throw from Valley Forge. The house was an old brick and stone farmhouse built early in the 20th century. The property, she explained, was owned by the Luden Coughdrop heir and was held in perpetuity as part of the Pennsylvania Nature Conservancy. Jeanne had permission to rent there as long as she pleased.

I rose early the next morning and sat in one of the lawn chairs in front of her house, sipping my coffee and enjoying the outdoors. The land sloped for several acres down to the road, which was obscured by an avenue of trees. Jeanne kept this huge area mowed with a tractor. Purple martins swooped in the air feasting on mosquitoes. At the bottom of the hill several deer were grazing. They took no notice of me sitting in the lawn chair, and Jeanne's dogs were so obviously used to deer that they ignored them. Live and let live seemed to be the prevalent attitude. In the distance were several receding lines of purplish mountains. Ever since leaving South

Carolina I'd generally followed the Appalachians, and Jeanne's house provided yet another view of that ancient and beautiful range.

Jeanne showed me around the "farm"—which she obviously deeply cared for. There were several big vacant outbuildings on the property and dense hardwood forests on two sides. It was a lovely, natural place. I felt happy it would never be developed. As we explored, Jeanne filled me in on what had been happening in her life. She'd recently had Lasik surgery and was thrilled to have 20-20 vision after wearing glasses for most of her life.

I explained that when I left there I planned to travel north of New York City to avoid the traffic and congestion. This one time I'd decided not to follow my usual rule of going through the middle of downtown. If truth be told, I felt intimidated by the idea of driving through such a huge metropolis. "Well, it would be just plain wrong not to see the greatest city of them all!" Jeanne chastened. She convinced me it would be just as easy, and much more interesting, to stay on I-95 right through Manhattan.

"I drive that route all the time," she assured me, "There's nothing to it." She wrote down directions to the Pennsylvania Turnpike, which hooked up with I-95, which led across the George Washington Bridge. "You'll have a fantastic view of the city skyline which is dominated by the Twin World Trade Towers. Then I-95 goes through the Bronx. You'll see the GW Bridge, the Twin Towers and the Bronx—all icons of Americana you shouldn't miss."

I knew she was right, so decided to bite the bullet, chance the traffic, and drive through the biggest city center of them all. Thank God Jeanne gave me that advice and I took it!

Most people think that Interstate 95, the most heavily traveled highway in the world, is one continuous 2,000 mile road that runs from Maine to Miami. At least that's what I thought—but it isn't precisely true. For a while in New Jersey, I-95 ceases to exist and drivers are funneled onto the New Jersey Turnpike, a toll road. Interstate 95 simply disappeared for a distance. I was a little lost as well as annoyed but kept following Jeanne's directions and hoping for the best, meanwhile passing through several tollbooths. This was the first time since leaving home that I had to pay a toll.

At one point on my drive between Philadelphia and New York, I became so befuddled that I pulled off the highway to figure it out on the map. Or rather, *try* to figure it out. No matter how many times I carefully moved my fingertip along the blue line that was I-95, the blue line simply vanished into a tangle of green, yellow and red threads. Then it reappeared. Then it disappeared again. I gave up and got back on whatever road I was on and continued to pay tolls while moving vaguely eastward and northward toward the city. Eventually I did indeed reach the magnificent George Washington Bridge across the Hudson River and got the promised look at the Manhattan skyline and Twin Towers.

I was glad I didn't avoid the city, no matter that this particular driving part of the trip was dreadful. Work crews were doing repairs as well as new construction all along the roadway, especially in and around Manhattan, and traffic often narrowed to one lane. Movement was stop and go. Those old freeways in and out of New York were the original American turnpikes built in the early fifties, and they were under-designed for the heavy usage of the 21st Century. What's more, I quickly discovered that New York drivers deserved their reputation for being discourteous; when someone needed to change lanes (a common occurrence), other drivers made no effort to accommodate. It sometimes seemed as if the New York drivers did everything possible to keep others *from* changing lanes. On the several occasions that I motioned a car with a blinking turn signal over in front of me, I got incredulous stares rather than the expected thank you wave.

Just before getting onto the George Washington Bridge, because no one would let me into the lane where I needed to be, I was forced onto an exit ramp and found myself on the narrow streets of Fort Lee, New Jersey. When I re-entered the interstate from Fort Lee, the toll taker took pity on my desperate pleas for direction and wrote down instructions on a slip of paper. She cautioned me in a Jamaican accent to *"stay in the lef lane, hahney, and don't ya ge'tout t'ovit for no reason!"* That, she assured me, would lead me to my destination, the New England Turnpike.

The trip through this mishmash of bumper-hugging traffic and torn-up asphalt was an exasperating experience. Thrilled as I was to be crossing the George Washington Bridge onto Manhattan Island and getting a look at America's most famous skyline, I couldn't look long or well because other cars were right on my tail and no one was shy about blasting their horn. Most of the traffic consisted of trucks and delivery vans, and it seemed as if our side mirrors were fractions of inches from each other. I was on the edge of my seat, expecting the crunch and shatter of a mirror breaking at any moment. I didn't dare swerve even the tiniest bit. If I lost a mirror I would have been driving half blind and the thought of that in such heavy, multi-lane traffic added to my anxiety.

After the GW, I went through five or six tunnel-like underpasses with trucks and cars still uncomfortably close on each side. Then suddenly I-95 became the Cross Bronx Expressway and for many miles passed through oceans of high rise apartment buildings. At best, the architecture of these projects was nondescript; at worst, ravaged. Spray-painted graffiti was everywhere. After what seemed like hours, I finally made it past the projects to the New England Turnpike and less traffic, but still plenty of road construction.

Along all these toll roads were rest plazas for travelers to stop for gasoline and food, etc. I stopped and purchased New York postcards, opting for the G. W. Bridge rather than the Twin Towers*. Then I continued on the 95 tollway into Connecticut, finally turning north onto non-toll I-91 at New Haven.

When I finally got to Vermont, there were hardly any cars on the road. Instead, I drove broad, well maintained highways through rolling green hills, past picturesque small towns with church steeples being the prominent feature. I became so mesmerized with the loveliness of Vermont that I missed my turn-off and had to backtrack almost twenty miles to catch 89-East. As soon as I drove across the Connecticut River I was beside the granite cliffs of New Hampshire. Soon I passed through Lebanon and 13 miles later reached the Grantham exit. I reached my son's house in Eastman about 6:30 PM.

Matt and Keri lived in a small house on a mountain in the New Hampshire woods. From the quiet of my solitary life, suddenly I was

---

* A decision I'd later regret!

part of a houseful of loud voices, laughter, kids, cats, dog, ferret, toys, music, books, and other general and friendly noise and clutter. We ate pizza for dinner, drank beer, and played a cutthroat game of Trivial Pursuit. I was assigned to sleep in the bunk below my step-granddaughter's bed, under lots of blankets, because in early September nights were already cold in New Hampshire. Tarzan, the golden retriever, curled onto the foot of the bed and helped keep my feet warm.

When I got to Matt and Keri's house, I had driven up the steep dirt driveway without giving it any thought. But next morning I realized the driveway might not be so easy to back down from. My Four Winds was a bit tail-heavy. Having decided I wanted her parked in a safer, more accessible location, Keri called directions as I carefully inched backwards down the driveway, fearful I would begin sliding at any moment. It was unavoidable but in the process the tailpipe was bent rather badly. It was another lesson learned the hard way. Never park a clumsy and un-svelte motor home where she can't get out as easily as she got in!

After getting the cumbersome RV down the steep driveway and situated on a flat spot across the road, Keri and I took her to Claremont to pick up the carpool for St. Mary's School. First, however, we had time for a bowl of scrumptious garlicky tomato bisque and a sandwich at the Original Boar's Head Restaurant.

We got to St. Mary's just as the three o'clock bell rang and kids came spilling out of the 100-plus year old redbrick building. Keri insisted we go inside to meet some of the teachers. The building itself reminded me of schools I went to as a child, with high ceilings, and hallways painted mossy green, light over dark. In Ariel's carpool were sisters Katie and Jennie. The girls were thrilled to ride home in a motorhome and giggled all the way.

I decided I liked almost everything about New Hampshire. I found the rugged, forested landscape incredibly lovely, and the people unpretentious and friendly. How can one not admire the "Live Free or Die" attitude embodied in the state motto? Plus, New Hampshire had neither income tax nor sales tax! The only negative might be the long, harsh winters. When Matt and Keri moved there from Texas in 1999, neither of them owned a winter coat, and Ariel had never before seen snow. Now they ice skated, cross country skied and claimed to love the snowy winters.

Ariel and her neighborhood friend Meg quickly turned the RV into their "playhouse." Matt, Keri, and I watched an HBO documentary, *One Year At Bellevue*, about life on the psychiatry ward at the famous New York City hospital. Matt said it was very much like his experience as a psychiatry resident at Dartmouth-Hitchcock Medical Center.

That weekend we visited the Hopkinton County Fair. I hadn't been to a fair since I was a teenager. Everything was the same except that they no longer had freak and girlie shows on the midway. Cotton candy and corn dogs, the agricultural and livestock exhibits, 4-H demonstrations and prizes, and of course the Midway of carnival games and barkers—nothing was changed. Matt and Keri picked the scariest ride they could find, the Zephyr, which looked like giant bullets twirling on a Ferris wheel. The "bullets" spun backward, forward, sideways and upside down. Matt and Keri got off the ride looking green but claiming it was great fun. Ariel and her pal settled for the Giant Swings.

In one long barn there were tables of homemade pies and cakes, breads and cookies, pickles, jams and home preserves, offered for competition by farm wives. In another barn were displays of woodcarving, weaving, quilting, basketry and so on. There were farmers selling maple syrup from their own trees, and others offering homemade white Vermont cheddar. We all pigged out on the goodies, then headed to the wildlife show about New England barred owls. After the lecture, Matt and Keri talked to the expert about Matt's attempts to attract inhabitants to the owl houses he'd built and nailed in the trees around their house. The ranger taught him how to stand under the trees and make owl sounds to call in the big birds. As soon as we got home, Matt went outside and began hooting and squawking but we saw no owls.

The next day Matt, Keri and Ariel went to climb Mooselac Mountain. They tried to talk me into joining them but I begged off. Climbing mountains (other than the metaphorical kind) no longer held much appeal. Staying home gave me a chance to do other things. After catching up my journal and doing three loads of laundry, I dug through the refrigerator and found ingredients for a white bean and sausage stew, which was simmering on the stove when the hungry mountain climbers returned. I'd also made a pan of cornbread. The simple meal was greatly appreciated by all.

The New Hampshire woods in early mid-September was spectacular to my eyes. Matt and Keri insisted that leaf-peeking hadn't really gotten a good start and I needed to stay another few weeks to catch it at its best, but I was ready to be back on the road. I felt I was already a little behind my non-schedule. After a nice visit with my son's family, I was eager to get back on the road. It was September 8th already!

Rain was predicted so I left early to avoid it. I drove through Concord, Boston and Providence, going right through the middle of the downtown areas. Traffic was brisk in Boston but nothing like New York City. Driving through Providence was a breeze. I'd thought about staying outside Providence and arranging a visit with my old high school friend, Beverly. Beverly had emailed and offered me the use of her townhouse. But as I drove through the city I realized it would probably be impossible to park an RV where Beverly lived; and you don't just show up at someone's door with such a large vehicle. Plus, after time spent in the midst of a busy, talkative family, I was ready for some alone time!

I reluctantly decided to by-pass Providence for the time being and continue down the Narragansett Peninsula where my cousin Emily lived in Saunderstown. It was an interesting drive. I ended up near Point Judith at Fisherman's Memorial State Park. This was one of the best camps I'd yet stayed and the cost was only $14 for a nice, private, level spot with full hookups.

Before hooking up, I went grocery shopping and cooked myself dinner. Then I telephoned Emily, figuring it was probably too late for a visit. But she said she was only 30 minutes away and would drive right over. About an hour later, she showed up. What a great surprise--we hadn't seen each other in thirty plus years! She taught kindergarten in a Providence inner city school and had just returned from Parent's Open House. She said that only a few parents had shown up. But Emily was a dedicated teacher determined to involve the parents and when I'd called she was in the process of telephoning each child's home to introduce herself and speak personally with a parent or guardian.

The weather was lovely but the mosquitoes were not, so we sat inside the RV and did our best in about two hours to catch up on all the years of separation. I hadn't actually seen Emily since visiting her family in Barrington the summer I was sixteen, and there was plenty of catching up to do. We spoke openly and honestly about our parents and about our eccentric grandmother. It was a conversation I could have had with no one else. We discussed family mysteries that we'd probably never figure out or understand. In spite of the long separation, we were able to be detached and open in expressing difficult truths. It was heartening to speak honestly with a cousin who shared some of the same DNA and who'd had similar experiences growing up.

Some years before Emily and Bob had lost their son Beau in an accident. That was a terrible tragedy they would never get over. Their other son, Jonathan, she told me, was doing extremely well, living in Connecticut with his young family and commuting to New York where he worked for Morgan Stanley. We promised to stay in touch and plan a family reunion so that our kids might get to know each other. We both admitted to feeling the scarcity of extended family in our lives. Then we hugged goodbye and went our separate ways.

The next day started better than it ended. Emily had suggested I take Route 1A back up the Narragansett coastline because it was more scenic than the road I'd driven down on. I took her advice and was so entranced with looking at the passing scenery that I missed the sign for Cape Cod. I had to backtrack (this was becoming a habit), but it was a nice drive, and I saw a lot more of the Rhode Island seashore than I otherwise would have. I bought gasoline at $1.79 a gallon (the most I'd yet had to pay) in the beautiful little village of Hamilton.

I crossed the Jamestown Bridge over Narragansett Bay to Conanicut Island and from there the Newport Bridge to Newport. I drove slowly through the streets and was able only to glimpse some of the mansions that line the Atlantic shore there. Then I followed Hwy 138 to the historic whaling port of Portsmouth and picked up the bigger Hwy 24 just past Island Park. At Fall River, which will forever be infamous for the 1892 Lizzie Borden ax murder, I got onto 195 and followed signs to Cape Cod.

Cape Cod was bigger than I thought and not what I expected. I drove alongside many cranberry and asparagus farms interspersed with small farming villages. I had thought it would be like the touristy atmosphere of coastal Florida but Cape Cod wasn't like that. I passed through Hyannis and then turned on Hwy 6 down the middle of the island. Eventually I reached the "elbow" to the very end, referred to as the "closed fist" because that's what it looks like on the map.

My plan was to stay overnight at an advertised campground about a mile from Provincetown, and the next day walk into town. I drove and drove but the more I drove, the more distant the end of the island seemed to be. I could swear it was longer than the advertised 65 miles. Finally, I reached my destination at dusk, and what a disappointment! The campground was unsightly and overpriced, with tiny, ill-equipped parking spaces and overhanging tree branches that scraped roughly against the roof. I was concerned an antenna might break off. Disgusted, I drove to another campground about seven miles back up the highway. At this facility, I was sent to a spot that required a 20-foot sewage hose and electric cord (mine were 12-feet). And if that weren't enough, a raucous group of senior citizens was seated in a circle of lawn chairs in the middle of the road drinking cocktails and trying to out-shout each other. Normally that wouldn't have bothered me. But by then I was tired, hungry and in no mood for loud drunks. Then what really got my goat was that the proprietor slapped a non-removable advertising sticker onto my windshield. No way was I staying there!

In a huff, I returned to the now pitch dark highway in hopes of finding yet another campground. I was about to give up and go to a motel when I spotted a small trailer sign pointing down a side road. I followed the road for several dark, deserted miles until I reached a gate leading into a graveled parking area. I knew if this place had room, I'd have to stay no matter what. There was a tiny, open-air booth office where a young woman sat reading a paperback novel under a dim light swirling with bugs. When I drove in, she looked up, surprised. "We can only offer you a temporary spot with electricity and water," she told me, "No sewage hookup." "I'll take it!" said I.

So that's how I ended up at an out of the way place with no clear idea where I was. There was no listing in my Trailer Life directory. There were only two other RVs in residence, both in a grove of trees across from the unpaved parking area and office. I had a quick, makeshift supper and watched what little TV I could pick up with my antenna. Nothing much on. Of course, there was no cable. One night cost $26, which was comparatively high, and they accepted cash only. I didn't care; I was exhausted and relieved to finally find a safe, quiet place to spend the night.

The next morning I slept late, had a banana and several cups of tea, and then proceeded to find out a little more about where I had mysteriously landed. It turned out to be quite a nice place. The campground occupied a huge acreage of undeveloped woodland. Among the trees were clearings for traditional tent camping. Since school was back in session only a few such campers were there. During the summer it stayed packed, I was told. There was a nice, modern shower and laundry facility a short walk down a dirt road. An elderly man from the big rig parked nearest me explained that the camp was equipped for only a few motorhomes, most of whom stayed the whole season. I was lucky to get a spot for the night because the people who had been in the place I was given had left that same morning for Florida. My neighbor explained he and his wife had been there since May and would soon leave to winter in south Texas. In several days the property was scheduled to close for the season.

He also told me that the park owners were an old Cape Cod family. The property the campground occupied was worth a fortune but by keeping it undeveloped, a natural area, they got tax breaks and were able to continue living there. The family resided year round in a modest house about a hundred yards behind the office. Four teenaged kids were in charge of all campground business and chores while the parents worked outside jobs.

The next day I spent puttering around and exploring the unusual place where I'd landed. It was a nice spot and I decided to sign up for another night. My plan was to next head to Maine for a quick visit with my friends Janice and Scott, and then backtrack to Catskill, New York to see another friend, Jane. I hoped to leave the RV at Jane's house in Catskill and go into Manhattan for a brief visit. Jane owned a townhouse in the West Village, so I was hoping we could go into the city and stay at her house. I also wanted to try again to visit Provincetown. Provincetown, a town brimming with history, was where the Pilgrims first stopped before making their final landfall at Plymouth in 1620.

I figured, what's the hurry? I had no one to please but myself—I was still getting used to that wondrous state of being. Even the frustrations of finding somewhere to stay on Cape Cod had serendipitously led me to this tranquil, out of the way location. I called my daughter in Houston to wish her a Happy Birthday and make sure she'd gotten the gift I sent. We had a nice chat and I climbed into my sleeping loft to read until finally nodding off sometime before midnight.

It was September 10, 2001.

CHAPTER 3

NINE ELEVEN

Next morning I woke around eight and went outside to sit at the picnic table and enjoy my coffee. It was the most beautiful New England day. Crisp weather, the birds were singing, trees were changing color and there wasn't a cloud in the sky. I was enjoying a second cup of coffee when my next door neighbor stuck his head out the door and shouted, "Turn on your television set. A plane just flew into The World Trade Center in New York."

I was in no hurry to go inside. I sat there for another few minutes then finally ambled back into the RV to get a banana. I nonchalantly clicked on the TV to check out what my neighbor found so newsworthy. Katie Couric and Matt Laurer were attempting to explain what had happened. Cameras zoomed in on smoke billowing from high in one of the Twin Towers. You couldn't really see much for the smoke. Everyone was suggesting that a small plane had gone off-course and the pilot had accidently flown into one of the buildings. Reporters were scrambling for facts. I was mildly interested, half watching The Today Show, sipping my coffee and munching a banana.

Then all of a sudden a jet zoomed across the sky from nowhere and smashed into the second World Trade Center Tower. At first I thought it was a video replay of the previous accident. It didn't look real. I watched in dawning horror as a huge fireball enveloped the upper floors of the second building, and suddenly understood that this was no accident—it was an attack. But by whom? And then I remembered the previous terrorist bombing of the World Trade Center parking garage in the early nineties. The scene playing out before my eyes on the television screen was incredulous. "Oh, my God, look. I can't believe this is really happening! Oh, my God, no!" Words spilled out of my mouth with no one to hear but myself. I was watching the impossible.

Reports came one after another. A third plane had crashed into the Pentagon in Washington. A fourth plane was down in Pennsylvania. There were unconfirmed reports of yet another hijacked plane. I sat stunned in front of the television. Katie and Matt were obviously shaken and uncertain but they forged on. Video of the second plane crashing into the South Tower played over and over. Fire and smoke poured from the windows and cameras zoomed in as big pieces of debris fell through the air. But it wasn't debris...it was people! Human beings were falling from a hundred floors up—you could see arms and legs flailing as they plummeted toward the earth. Why would people be falling? Then it dawned on me that they were jumping—they were choosing quick and certain doom over the slow and excruciating death of being burned alive. I was watching this horror happen on television in real time! Ordinary people who had gone to work that morning with only the most mundane things on their minds had suddenly been confronted with the unimaginable!

On TV one conjecture followed another, the truth as uncertain and unbelievable as the wildest rumors. Like millions of others across the nation, I sat mesmerized before the television screen. That's how it began. Then suddenly I thought of loved ones far away, wondering where they were, if they knew, if they were safe, what else could be happening, and particularly *what would happen next?* I tried my cell phone but all circuits were jammed. I tried calling South Carolina, New Hampshire and Texas. No luck. Every time I hit redial all I got was a fast busy signal.

I was still watching live television coverage when the second tower began to collapse. Like one of those carefully orchestrated skyscraper implosions I'd seen on television, the massive World Trade Tower Building crumpled in upon itself, creating a gigantic nebula of rubble, ash and smoke that billowed like a tsunami of detritus onto the streets of New York, swallowing everything in a monstrous, churning, nasty cloud.

"Many firemen and policemen are being buried alive in their rescue attempts," Matt Lauer spoke in a controlled monotone. "*We are watching thousands die....*"

"Twenty-five floors in that building belong to the brokerage firm of Morgan Stanley," mentioned Katie, and suddenly my mind rushed to Emily who only nights earlier had proudly told me about her son Jonathan and his job at Morgan Stanley. *He might be dead,* I thought. *Perhaps I just watched him die.* Or...maybe he was in the other tower or not there...or.... My thoughts jumped from one possibility to another. I knew so few specifics. Time moved in slow motion. Then incredibly the other tower began to fall. And again, I watched awe struck with disbelief and horror.

The television remained on all day. In late afternoon I was finally able to get through to Jim on my cell phone. Like me, he'd watched everything as it happened and had stayed glued to the TV. When I finally reached Leslie in Houston, she said they had closed the school where she taught. She'd had to call parents to pick up their children, although many came before being called. Todd also had been evacuated from his high rise office building downtown. Houston was on "high alert" as a possible target.

It took even longer before I reached Keri and learned that Matt was still on 36-hour rotation at Dartmouth-Hitchcock Hospital. There were news reports that medical personnel in New York were preparing for a massive influx of the injured; triage centers were being set up and doctors and nurses from across the nation were volunteering to go there and help. People were lining up everywhere to donate blood.

It was after 8 PM before I finally talked to my friend Janice in Maine. She was expecting me in Columbia Foreside the next day but we agreed this was no time to visit. She was concerned about her daughter in New York; she hadn't yet heard from her. "I don't believe she was near the towers but I'll worry till I talk to her and know for sure that she's okay," she said. It was almost impossible to get calls in or out of New York City. I tried again to telephone Emily but still couldn't get through. I was horrified at what she might be going through—whether Jonathan was okay. I assumed he'd been at work in the Morgan Stanley office in the South Tower. I was dismayed at how thoroughly cell phone communication was disrupted.

I watched television until late that night, unable to peel myself away from the nonstop news coverage. There were still few facts to go on. Just that two hijacked planes had crashed separately into each of the World Trade Towers in what was certainly an orchestrated attack. I was doubly glad I had taken Jeanne's advice to drive through New York instead of avoiding it. I was thankful to have seen those iconic skyscrapers dominating the Manhattan skyline during the last weeks of their existence.

Another hijacked passenger jet had flown directly into the Pentagon and many hundreds were dead and wounded there, also. And a fourth hijacked airliner had crashed into a field in Pennsylvania, everyone on board killed. That crash was a huge mystery still. Reports suggested it was on a heading toward Washington.

President Bush soon grounded all air traffic over the United States. There I was below one of the busiest air corridors in the world and the skies were absolutely empty and quiet. Very little traffic moved even on the ground. The silence was strange. But the murmur of TV news droned on and on, the same stories repeated; it seemed everyone was waiting for "what next?" Were we at war? If so, with whom? Who did this to us? Why? Nothing made sense.

The opinion of a few Washington insiders was that this was probably the work of the radical Muslim terrorist Osama bin Laden. I'd never heard of him! Experts said that using jetliners as weapons had his fingerprints all over it. Some people began wondering aloud if courageous passengers on United Flight 93 might have caused it to crash rather than reach its target in D. C.—the Capitol Building or White House? Hard information was nonexistent but that didn't stop speculation. I finally forced myself to turn off the television and crawl under the covers in my sleeping loft. But sleep wouldn't come;

my mind still hummed with shock, sadness, anger and disbelief. It was the first time I'd felt unhappily alone. I wanted to talk to another human about what had happened, to try somehow to make sense of it.

The next morning I wasn't sure what to do or where to go. I thought I might have to give up my journey and go home. The other two RVs and I stayed where we were for the time being. Announcements on local radio and television said that the highway patrol wanted people on the Cape to stay put unless it was absolutely necessary to leave. Interstate 95, the main corridor between Boston and New York, was on high alert and unnecessary traffic was being discouraged. All airline travel had been cancelled. So I figured, oh well, where better to be "stuck" than Cape Cod? Finally, though, we had to leave because the campground was closing. By then there was only me and one other RV. The owners suggested we try another spot just off Route 6 several miles up the road near Wellfleet. So that's where I headed.

First thing in the morning I flipped on the TV and it stayed on all day. I'd never been much of a TV watcher but it was almost impossible to pull myself away from the nonstop coverage. Reports were that no traffic moved in Manhattan, no vehicles crossed the bridges and no one was allowed to drive through the tunnels. Todd's sister, Traci, lived on the Lower East Side in Manhattan. Todd had finally spoken with her and learned that the area around her apartment was a mess. Traci was staying inside because the air outside was still choked with soot and ash. When her office shut down soon after the disaster, she could get no transportation home and had to spend the night with a friend near work. The next morning she walked more than twenty blocks through dirty haze to return home.

The tragedy was far worse than the bombing of the Oklahoma City Federal Building. It was worse than Pearl Harbor! There was talk in Congress of a Declaration of War but no one seemed to know who to declare war against. There was no specific identifiable enemy, just obscure "terrorists." I wasn't even sure what a "terrorist" was. Not that I was uninformed—I read a daily newspaper, subscribed to a weekly news magazine and tried to catch the news each evening on television. But I didn't have a clear idea of who the people were who hated America so much they wanted to destroy us. The word jihad wasn't yet in my vocabulary. It was the most incomprehensible of situations.

I felt immensely fortunate that I'd seen the Towers with my own eyes such a short time before their destruction. I had quickly forgotten the superficial aspects of my life and for the time being lived each day listening to the news and not giving much thought to what I would do or where I should go next. Nothing seemed worth thinking about except what was happening each moment. The future had suddenly become nebulous.

I wasn't the only one feeling this way. When I'd thought about what might happen on my trip, my wildest imagination hadn't conjured anything like this. Suddenly everything was changed. I quit the travel writing in my journal and instead described the larger picture of what I saw and heard about the attacks on America. When I first wrote bin Laden's name I had no idea how to spell it. I thought he was Ben Lauden. The attacks of September 11 had become the compass from which, for the time being, I measured and described everything.

For all the news being broadcast, factual information remained scanty. Thousands of people were dead—reporters threw around estimates between two and twenty thousand. All that was known for sure was that a group of mid-eastern Islamic terrorists had carefully planned and carried out the hijacking of four large passenger planes fully loaded with jet fuel. They had turned the planes into suicide/homicide bombs and used them to target places they apparently thought would symbolically most hurt America. Three "bombs" hit their targets. Where the fourth "bomb" was headed might never be known. No one yet knew what had caused the fourth airliner to crash. Either the brave crew and/or passengers had sacrificed all to thwart a larger disaster, or the incompetent terrorist pilot had flown the plane into the ground. We had learned that many passengers on the fourth plane were in cell phone communication with loved ones and therefore aware what had happened in New York and Washington. I wanted to believe they'd taken matters into their own hands. I hoped the full story of United Flight 93 would eventually come out.

Lots of rumors flew. Journalistic sensationalism obscured facts. With so little new or substantiated to report, the media resorted to repetition and hyperbole. The story became them telling the story. Therefore I was finally able to drag myself away from the television.

After a few days, cell phones were once again reliable. I was finally able to make calls and inform others of changed plans. I realized it probably wasn't the best time to visit Maine. I called Jane in New York because I was supposed to go there when I left Jan's house. There was no answer at Jane's house in the city. I knew she lived fairly close to the World Trade Center but had no idea how close. I finally reached her at a house she'd recently bought in Catskill, New York. On 9-11 Jane had been in Catskill and now authorities were not allowing anyone back into Manhattan. Jane said she'd checked with her neighbors on Hudson Street and everyone assured her the house was okay. The streets outside her door were full of debris but there was no real damage where she lived. Her address was fifteen blocks from what was now being called "Ground Zero." "My house is inside the yellow tape," she said. "That means residents need a special pass to enter the area."

"I'll bet you're glad you were in the country when it happened," I suggested. She vehemently responded, "No! I am NOT glad! It is MY house and MY city and I wish I were there right now. I can't wait to get back!"

Was that really me who groused on the first night about disliking Cape Cod? Goes to show how getting to know a place—even a little— can completely change a person's mind. I quickly decided I could not have been "stuck" in more pleasant or interesting surroundings. The new campground where I'd landed wasn't nearly as secluded and nice as the first but it was fine. The owner told the few campers there to stay as long as we needed, just be sure to clean up before leaving. Nine-eleven seemed to have brought out the best and most generous in everyone I had contact with.

For the next several days I drove to the Wellfleet Harbor each morning. There was a large parking area there with not many cars. Then I wiled away many hours exploring the beautiful little historic town. There was a big estuary/salt flat on one side of the harbor, with trails through a wild bird preserve. The town itself was small enough to easily walk from one end to the other. Along the streets were numerous art studios and galleries, most of them open to the public. I soon learned that Wellfleet's historic claim to fame had been their whaling, fishing and oyster fleets; modern day Wellfleet was best known as an artist's colony and summer resort. I loved it there!

The weather was ideal, about 65 sunny degrees during the day with pleasantly cool nights. Tourist season had ended and I was there at the perfect time. The beach was almost deserted, pebbly and pleasant to walk on. I picked up several pieces of sea glass which I added to my growing collection of souvenirs. There were a few European tourists sunbathing in bikinis even though I felt comfortable in a sweater. In the afternoon the restaurants were packed. Local specialties were the famous Wellfleet oyster and New England lobster roll. Of course I sampled both and found them outstanding.

I also discovered a stationary shop crammed with all kinds of paper and writing instruments, journals, albums and cards. My kind of place! There was also a great secondhand bookstore. The owner left the shop open even when he wasn't there and purchases were made on the honor system. I wrote down the book I bought and left money in a shoebox.

Meanwhile the tragedy of 9-11 played out without letup in the media. I walked into a pottery studio and the artist wasn't there but he'd placed a black wreath on the door and left the radio babbling its tragic reportage. Later someone told me that the studio belonged to a Quaker who was vehemently anti-war and violence.

One day I drove to Provincetown and found the streets jammed with people. There was still plenty of tourism and commercialization there, and lots of rainbow flags. Provincetown, one of the oldest settlements in America and originally settled by Portuguese fishermen, had become an iconic gay destination. I wasn't expecting to see so many tee shirt shops and quaint B & B's. It had definitely been discovered by the trendy "out" crowd.

I also visited North Truro where many painters have lived and worked, among them the great Edward Hopper. In Truro I found pristine white beaches with cottages nestled among the nearby dunes. I'd never seen such high dunes! The September sunlight was clear and shimmering, a major attraction for the artists in the area. In the late afternoon I walked along the ocean's edge. To the northeast, the silhouette of Provincetown was clearly visible rising out of the sea.

As the sun approached the horizon, more people wandered onto the beach at Truro, many with cameras. I settled myself against a sand dune and enjoyed what came next. That evening's sunset was spectacular: clear blue sky slowly mutating to turquoise to green to yellow to orange to coral to lavender to deep shades of violet. I regretted leaving my camera in the camper but was unwilling to miss even a moment of the spectacle in order to run back and get it. Instead, I decided to return the next evening better prepared.

The following afternoon I went back to the same spot on North Truro beach and waited for sundown. I had a new roll of color film in my Minolta and could hardly wait for the show to begin. It began as a replay of the previous.... An almost deserted beach, then as dusk approached the arrival of audience. But the second night's performance turned out to be a weak replay of the previous night's show. The sunset had the same general color spectrum but without equal intensity. I snapped photos anyway and felt grateful that I'd at least once seen the spectacle at its most glorious.

One thing that I particularly liked about the area around Truro and Wellfleet was that it seemed unsullied in comparison with other beach communities I'd visited. There was no overbuilding, not one single high rise and no condominiums. I was grateful that parts of Cape Cod had resisted the over-development of other American seashores. For the most part it still had a small town character and charm.

After a week on Cape Cod, I was smitten. If I'd spent only one night as planned, then I would never have discovered Wellfleet or North Truro. Everything would have been judged through the glitzy lens of Provincetown. As it was, my forced interlude on Old Cape Cod became one of the highlights of my trip.

I finally managed to pull myself away from that beautiful island. But before leaving, I took one last stroll along the boardwalk in Wellfleet, crossing the salt marshes. An elderly man in tattered jeans and rubber boots was wading in the muck, collecting seaweed. He looked up and smiled. "I harvest this for my garden," he explained. "It makes wonderful fertilizer." I smiled back and walked on. A woman standing at the end of the boardwalk spoke to me. "Do you know who that is?" she asked. "No," I answered. "He said he was harvesting seaweed to put in his garden." "That is Howard Zinn you were talking to," she informed me. "Who is Howard Zinn?" I asked. "He's a world renowned historian and author. Professor emeritus at Boston University," she explained. I had never heard of Howard Zinn.

Then another coincidence happened. As I drove away from the Cape listening to NPR, there was an interview about the terrorist attacks and what America's response should be. The interview was with Howard Zinn. He was saying that President Bush and Congress should not rush into war, that war would solve nothing and might possibly make matters worse. He advised a cautious and thoughtful response that wouldn't lead into a long, drawn out stalemate of hostilities.

I drove into the middle of Massachusetts, NPR continuing to play on the radio with non-stop commentary about September 11. Every commentator had a different viewpoint and few seemed to be in agreement with others. I could see rifts already starting to form between "hawks" who advised the immediate bombing of terrorist strongholds and "doves" who advised not answering violence with more violence. Every "expert" had a different take on what the US should or shouldn't do. Plus, these "experts" were in great disagreement over specifically who "the enemy" was. For certain it was "terrorists"—al Qaeda (never heard of them either)—the Taliban (?)—and maybe it was Saddam Hussein or Osama bin Laden or.... The list went on.

Finally I was able to reach my cousin Emily by cell phone and she had the best possible news. Jonathan was safe! I also spoke with Jane. She had finally been allowed home to her beloved house on

Hudson Street. She described her neighborhood as "in the war zone." "I have a pass that gets me in and out of my street," she said.

I hated not being able to visit her but all my plans were now necessarily changed. So instead of continuing west or east I followed the highway north into Massachusetts and let the road take me where it would.

CHAPTER 4

NORTHBOUND

That night I stayed near Northampton. Before settling in, however, I checked out the town. What I found was a New England college town with one long main street bustling with students. There was lots of long hair and backpacks. On the edge of downtown was the beautiful campus of Smith College.

It was in Northampton that I began to notice American flags displayed in yards, on storefronts and on cars. The overt patriotism was apparently a spontaneous reaction to the terrorist attacks—even in a liberal college town. If the terrorist's intentions had been to dishearten Americans, it looked as if they'd accomplished the opposite. War, a concept that was repugnant and unthinkable only a few days before, now seemed a real possibility.

In spite of continuing obsession with the events of Nine Eleven, I enjoyed the college towns of Massachusetts. In Amherst I visited an old cemetery and came across the grave of Emily Dickinson. A nice woman volunteered to take my picture there. Then I drove down Main Street until I found the Dickinson homestead. When I reached the house, I joined a guided tour that was just beginning. We were an unusual mix of people in the group, some students, a family of Germans, me and a few others. The tour took more than an hour and was led by a very knowledgeable and informative guide. I stood in the upstairs bedroom and stared out the window through the same panes of glass at the same general scene that Emily Dickinson must have looked upon thousands of times. I thought about how her best poetry was written in that austere little bedroom where I stood.

In her lifetime, few people knew that Dickinson wrote poetry. Her father detested what he referred to as "loud, literary women" and so she kept her endeavors to herself. Only after Emily had completed a long day of housework and cooking did she retreat to her bedroom and compose those astonishing poems. During her lifetime only two badly edited poems were published. Today she would probably be diagnosed as depressed, given a prescription for Prozac and "cured." Being in her house—*in her very bedroom!*—touched me deeply.

I had finally begun to achieve a steady routine. It had been more than three weeks since leaving home. The terrorist attacks had caused a disruption, and before that I was still in "uncertain" mode. Those first weeks I always had to check lists and charts of what to do and when to do it every time I hooked up or unhooked the RV. Now I set up and broke down connections quickly, finally trusting myself not to forget anything. Every day felt more at ease and at home.

My main frustration was that with the time it took to plan, then drive from place to place, eat meals, take showers (a much slower process than home), sightseeing, connecting and disconnecting, and keeping clothes and other gear clean and stowed, I hadn't actually gotten much writing done. I kept up with my journal but had only written a little other than that.

I drove contentedly along Massachusetts State Road 2, otherwise known as the Mohawk Trail, which meandered through hilly, forested country dotted with small towns and farms. In the far northwest corner of the state was North Adams, an old textile village where the mills were as deserted as those in South Carolina—the jobs moved to cheaper labor overseas. The state had taken one huge empty factory near downtown and renovated it into the Massachusetts Museum of Contemporary Art (called MassMoCA).

Searching for MassMoCA, I pulled into a McDonald's with flag flying at half-mast above the golden arches. I needed to study my map. Across the street was a Congregational Church with a sign on the marquee inviting guests to a special service commemorating September 11, and people were streaming in. I felt like joining the people but let my shyness (and jeans and tee shirt) keep me from it. Too bad; I wish I'd gone.

MassMoCA was only a few blocks away, so I headed that direction. There were only a few cars in the parking lot. Leading into the museum was a long row of upside down trees, their huge pots suspended from cables. It was such a strange sight that it took me a minute to figure out what I was looking at. The special exhibit inside was titled "Games and Art." It was interesting but also partly pretentious. One of Yoko Ono's "art works" consisted of a big stretched canvas with hundreds of nails randomly hammered into it, the hammer dangling from a chain off to the side. What was that? My first thought was that it was "interactive art"—I rather liked the idea—in which gallery visitors could hammer their own nail into the "work in progress." But, no, there was also a prominent placard warning, "*Do Not Touch!*" I must not have been the only one with the interactive idea. I wondered what (if?) the museum had paid Yoko for that "work of art"? That got me to thinking about what "art" was and even more so, what it wasn't.

Something that I particularly liked about the museum was the building itself. The industrial architecture with its high ceilings, factory windows and elevated steel walkways worked perfectly as a showcase for contemporary art. Parts of the framework looked as if it had been constructed by a giant, old-fashioned toy erector set. The brickwork with its rich patina and geometric patterns was one of the most striking "artworks" on display. No matter what I saw in the museum, my eyes were pulled back to those wonderful old brick walls.

In North Adams I passed through neighborhoods with two and three-story houses lined up like stair steps along hillside streets. Many of the houses were flying American flags. I wondered if there was a reason for the flags other than yet another example of patriotic fervor resulting from the September 11 attacks. North Adams seemed particularly patriotic.

I stopped for lunch at "Linda's Café," an unpretentious eatery near downtown. I ordered the day's special which was corned beef hash and eggs with whole wheat toast and a homemade blueberry muffin. The food was excellent and cost a grand total of $4.80, coffee included.

I next headed west on Interstate 90 into New York state, and before the day was over had passed through Albany, Schenectady, Utica and Syracuse. Later I couldn't remember which city was which. The day ended at Cayuga Lake State Park near Seneca Falls. It was a pretty area in the Finger Lakes district. After getting hooked up and settled for the night, I once again sat mesmerized in front of the television. Media reporting of the terrorist attacks was still the only thing on the three main channels. Not that there was anything new to report—the same stories were repeated and the same images shown, but it was hard not to watch.

The next day I drove along Cayuga Lake until I reached Seneca Falls, another typical northeastern town. As I drove down Fall Street, I noticed a sign for The National Women's Rights Hall of Fame. I parked at a pizza restaurant several blocks away and walked back to the museum. Along the way I passed several children selling Kool Aid from a sidewalk drink stand in front of their house. The homemade sign read, "For Sale for the American Red Cross." Of course I bought a cup.

The Hall of Fame was dedicated to the women who in the early twentieth century had worked under nearly impossible circumstances to gain the most basic civil rights for half the American population. Although most people think the right to vote was the only reason for the Women's Movement, the reasons were actually much broader. The Suffragist's Crusade also strove for the right of women to own property, to keep their own wages and to have equal guardianship of children after divorce. Black men had these rights fifty years before women of any race did. Today most Americans are incredulous that such gender inequality was tolerated. Visiting the museum made me feel grateful that an extraordinary group of women in the small village of Seneca, New York, had had the vision, the courage and the persistence to challenge the massive inequities of their time.

After leaving Seneca Falls, I drove back roads until reaching Lake Ontario. Along the way, I passed many farms with bright yellow crops in the fields and fruit orchards of apples and peaches. I saw a number of Mennonite farmers who were dressed similarly to the Amish. The Mennonites, however, were using modern machinery. I saw Mennonite men driving pickup trucks, tractors and harvesters.

At Clyde, New York I crossed the Erie Canal. If there hadn't been a sign, I'd have thought it was just a large culvert. The Canal's humble appearance belied what an amazing engineering feat it was in the early nineteenth century, and what a huge role it played in the settling of America. The Canal is 363 miles long with 83 locks that navigate an elevation change of 500 feet between the Hudson River and Lake Erie. Originally it was only 40 feet wide and four feet deep but eventually was enlarged to 70 and seven. This important waterway was crucial in opening the Midwest to mass trade and settlement by connecting the harbor of New York City with the Great Lakes. It was dug mostly by manual and mule labor.

That night I settled at a quiet campground on Indian Creek near Hartland, NY. I was seeing more American flags as I passed through small towns. I also began seeing flags attached to cars and trucks. It was a phenomenon that had seemingly sprung up without suggestion or plan. I hadn't heard a word about it on television or radio. In upstate New York I saw flags everywhere and wondered if the same thing were happening all over the country.

I was getting used to the RV lifestyle. Even though alone, I wasn't lonely. There was too much to do and see. One of the discussions on radio was about an epidemic of sleeplessness across America because people had been so frightened by the terrorist attacks. But after an initial few nights of restlessness, I was sleeping better than I ever had. Each day I woke and went to bed by my own natural inclination. During the day I got plenty of physical exercise and at night I slept soundly and well.

At the Hartland RV park, I cleaned the Four Wind's holding tanks, then showered and sat down to a bowl of just-picked organic peaches purchased the previous day at an orchard road stand. After de-camping I got directions to a nearby propane dealer and had that tank topped off. The nights were getting cold and I had to use the furnace quite a lot. After getting propane, I crossed the Erie Canal again and was struck anew by what a humble waterway it is to occupy such a momentous place in American history.

My next destination was Niagara Falls. Somehow I made a wrong turn and instead ended up at Fort Niagara. Fort Niagara was built by the French in the early 1700's as an Indian outpost. I got out and had a look around. Across the river I saw Canada for the first time. A nice young couple said they were headed toward the falls and offered to let me follow them. I followed them through the charming Canadian border town of Lewiston, NY. After a while, they broke away while pointing me toward signs that led the rest of the way. I parked at a nearby motel and walked from there to the falls.

I had no preconceptions and found Niagara Falls amazing. It was where my maternal great-grandparents had spent their honeymoon and they were still talking about it when they died more than fifty years later. I don't think anyone in the family had visited there since. What I found was a beautiful rainbow arcing over the crashing spray, and the sound was immense. The hydroelectric power generated by the falls provides much of upstate New York with electricity. A hot air balloon was floating overhead with a big I Love NY logo on it. I didn't stay long because I was running late and wanted to get back on the highway. I hiked back to the RV, bought some tacky postcards inside a shopping mall attached to the motel and pointed the RV south.

My plans were to cross into Canada at Niagara and follow the Trans Canadian Highway north and west around the Great Lakes. However, radio announcements warned that the wait to cross the border was running about eleven hours! The Canadian-U.S border was normally one of the most open in the world with virtually no delay, but because of 9-11 security had been increased to the highest level. A huge backup of traffic was stalled on each side of the border as agents thoroughly searched every vehicle. Forget that!

Okay, here's something I've avoided discussing so far. I've often been asked if I took a gun on my trip. The answer is yes I did. Of course I had no intentions of taking it out of its hiding place unless absolutely necessary. Knowing it was tucked away but accessible offered a layer of security that I wouldn't have otherwise had. I had a license for the gun and knew how to use it. My job as private investigator required that I carry a gun in my car. I wasn't about to let a Canadian border guard confiscate my trusty Baretta! I u-turned and followed the road signs back to Interstate 90.

For the rest of that afternoon I followed I-90 southwesterly along Lake Ontario and Lake Erie, paying tolls at regular intervals. I drove through Buffalo and Rochester, then quickly passed through the northwestern tip of Pennsylvania and into Ohio. When I left New York the tolls dropped from $8 to 65 cents!

As I drove, I thought about how contented I was. For the most part, I'd been successful at "staying in the moment." Everything I passed, everything I saw, for me it was all new. Sometimes I put music in the CD player and sometimes I went back to listening to the 9-11 news that dominated almost every radio station. Mostly, though, I drove in silence by the woods, lakes and villages, taking it all in.

CHAPTER 5

INTO THE HEARTLAND

By late afternoon I'd settled into a campground across the road from Lake Erie. The lake was like a huge calm ocean. From previous reading I'd formed a mental picture of the Great Lakes as polluted but Lake Erie looked clean and healthy. I was on the outskirts of Geneva-on-the-Lake, Ohio, a resort town made up of motels and lake houses strung along the shore; most looked as if they'd been built in the forties and fifties. The overall effect was charming. It felt a little as if I'd stepped back in time.

All the next day I stuck with I-80 and 90, mostly toll roads, in order to make time. Vehicles of all sizes zoomed past me. Everyone seemed to be exceeding the posted speed limits of 65 to 75 MPH. From the Interstate it looked like America was in a big hurry.

I soon passed through Cleveland and crossed the Cuyahoga River, famous for being so polluted that it caught fire in 1969 and helped to inspire the environmental movement. The Cuyahoga, cleaned up and again supporting aquatic life, flowed like any normal river, no longer "oozing" with the industrial run-off of its past. I drove SR 303 for a while, taking a straight and hilly secondary highway that led south from Cleveland to Brunswick. That gave me an opportunity to see the Ohio countryside away from big city congestion. In Brunswick, I stopped at Camper World to try to get my bent back steps fixed but the service department was already overbooked.

After leaving Brunswick and re-entering the interstate on the outskirts of Cleveland, there was a big interchange with signs pointing one way to Columbus and the other way to Toledo. Since I had little knowledge of Ohio geography, I had no idea which way to go! I had to exit the freeway in a busy area in order to study a map. Turns out I needed to take the Toledo route. I didn't like the in-city traffic with cars speeding here and there, people changing lanes, everyone knowing exactly where they were going and in a hurry. Lesson to myself: always figure out which roads and loops you need to take before getting into the middle of big cities!

West of Cleveland, the landscape became rural, with crop fields stretching to the horizon on both sides of the road. The scenery was pleasantly monotonous for many miles. I passed through the midsized city of Toledo, then westward through more flat farmland, and finally entered Indiana. I stopped that night at Elkhart, which is where my motorhome had been built. On billboards leading into town Elkhart advertised itself as the "RV Capital of America" and also as the "Band Instrument Capital of the World."

On radio and television, focus was still on the 9-11 disaster. Commentators talked of an epidemic of national angst but for me everything and every day was a new, different and meaningful experience. Everywhere I went seemed peaceful and prosperous. The weather could not have been more pleasant. It was a stressful time in America at large but within me all was calm. It was a peculiar juxtaposition of which I was very aware.

I traveled on the interstates (no more tolls to pay) in order to make better time across the big states of the Midwest. I traversed Gary and Chicago as quickly as possible. The traffic there was heavy and roads were bumpy with potholes. As in other large cities, road construction was ubiquitous and often slowed traffic to a crawl. The heart of Chicago was hidden from the freeway and I wished I'd seen more. Once I got past the city, I was surprised at how agricultural Illinois was. I crossed the Mississippi River on the Twin Bridges: Moline, East Moline and Rock Island, Illinois on one side; Davenport, Iowa on the other.

Iowa looked just as I thought it would: flat and open with cornfields stretching as far as the eye could see. In the distance, I noticed plenty of two-story farmhouses, red barns and grain silos. Interstate 80 was absolutely level and straight, and the traffic was sparse and speedy. Eighteen wheelers with American flags whipping from antennae zoomed past me at more than 80 miles an hour. At Des Moines I turned right toward Ames. It seemed like everything in Iowa was laid out in neat square grids. I was headed to Ames to visit my friend Sheryl, who of all my friends seemed the least likely to live in Iowa. She taught English at Iowa State University.

I got to Sheryl's house a few minutes before she and Paul returned from work so I sat in my motorhome, opened a diet coke and watched CNN. Sheryl's boyfriend Paul was from England and taught medieval British history at the university. For dinner that night they took me to a Peruvian restaurant in downtown Ames. A small town in Iowa was an unusual place for my first taste of the cuisine of Peru. Whatever, it was delicious. Then we rushed back to Sheryl's house to listen to President Bush address the nation. As the president spoke words full of patriotic fervor and determination to destroy Al Qaeda and the Taliban, Paul could hardly contain his anger. He muttered a steady stream of invective against both Bush and Prime Minister Tony Blair who was seated on the podium behind Bush. Sheryl and I didn't say much. I wanted to believe that our leaders knew what they were doing.

After the address, I suddenly realized that my purse was missing. Had I left it at the restaurant? My heart did a flip-flop. Sheryl drove me back downtown but the restaurant was closed. What a sinking feeling to think that your money and credit cards are missing! *Okay, just deal with it*, I thought. When we got back to Sheryl's, Paul met us at the door holding up my purse. I breathed a huge sigh of relief. When we'd pulled the living room chairs closer around the television set, we'd covered my purse with a chair. Then when Paul moved the chairs back, there it was.

Next morning, Sheryl and I sat in her back yard drinking strong New Orleans coffee and talking about people we knew and places we missed. She gave me a progress report on the memoir she was writing about growing up in New Orleans (since published as *Swampsongs*). She talked about how much she missed the South, particularly Louisiana. She had a tenured position at Iowa State and

Ames was a wonderful small town, et cetera, et cetera...she didn't have a negative thing to say. But she just couldn't escape how alien it felt there.

Sheryl said her relationship with Paul was stormy and hinted that it would probably soon end. She was dealing with several difficult issues. She'd been diagnosed with Hepatitis C, a disease she admitted resulted from youthful indiscretions. "No one to blame but myself," she said. For a while she'd had to inject herself with interferon and the interferon or the disease—or both—had caused deafness in one ear. She spoke of her illness in a regretful but accepting manner.

Then she changed the subject to her large Cajun family. Sheryl was full of funny and painful stories and it was obvious she missed them dearly. She had a PhD and five or six published books of critically acclaimed poetry, yet she was the only one of her siblings to go beyond high school. She said she yearned to return to the South but was disinclined to leave a tenured professorship. We talked for several hours and it was hard to pull myself away, but it was time to get back on the road. Reluctantly I took my leave

I'd driven only several blocks when the convex attachment to my side mirror suddenly fell off. I pulled into the nearest parking lot, which happened to be a kidney dialysis center, and was able to retrieve the unbroken mirror from the middle of the road. I super-glued it back on and drove straight to an auto parts store where I purchased a replacement. Without convex side mirrors it was difficult to see in back as the RV had no rearview mirror. My large side mirrors were all important! Small maintenance problems happened almost daily and had to be dealt with immediately.

From Ames it was a quick trip back to Des Moines where I hooked up with the Interstate west toward Omaha. More miles of flat Iowa farmland passed by. Then at Council Bluffs I crossed the Missouri River and on the other side was Nebraska. Omaha was then a short drive away. I telephoned Mike at his camera store and got directions to a large mall. I waited in the parking lot only a short time before Mike showed up and led me to the home where he and Suzi have lived since the late sixties. My first impression of Omaha was of a nice and orderly, All-American city. Also, once across the river, the flatland had changed to hilly terrain. Omaha had plenty of trees and hills.

Mike had to return to work but Suzi had plans for a full day of sightseeing. She took me on a tour of the city and our first destination was Boys' Town, not far from Mike and Suzi's house.

I was surprised at the large size of Boy's Town—now officially called Boy's and Girl's Town. My first impression was that it bore little resemblance to the movie orphanage in which Spencer Tracy portrayed Father Flanagan. First, we drove through agricultural plots where the kids farmed their own produce. Then we passed through a neighborhood of large modern homes. Suzi explained that these were group homes occupied by boys or girls and their house parents. We next entered an impressive campus of many buildings including classrooms, a theater and music conservatory, fine arts facility, athletic stadium, playing fields and a Hall of History Museum. We observed teams of both boys and girls practicing soccer and a group of boys doing football drills. Suzi said that Boys Town teams compete in sports with Nebraska public schools, and many of the residents go to college with athletic and academic scholarships.

Suzi also pointed out vocational ed facilities where the kids learn such skills as auto mechanics and construction trades. When each resident of Boys' Town reaches the age of 18, he or she is sent into the world with a good education as well as an employable job skill.

The next day Jim flew to Omaha from Greenville and his plane arrived 20 minutes early into an airport that was nearly deserted. Many travelers had cancelled flights or quit flying altogether since 9-11 and the airport was as empty as if it were the middle of the night instead of what should have been the busiest time of day. Large numbers of planes were still grounded. Before we could enter the airport gates, a policeman motioned us over and thoroughly searched Suzi's car. It was a new experience. *This is America?* I wondered. The huge airport parking areas were almost devoid of cars.

When Mike returned from work that afternoon, we sat outside in the perfect autumn weather and visited with friends and relatives who dropped by. Both Mike and Suzi came from Omaha pioneer families and they seemed to know everyone in town. Lots of their neighbors had lived in the same houses since they were built in the 1960's. One of Mike's cousins lived in the house that backed up to his. It was an atmosphere like many towns used to have but not so many anymore. Omaha seemed truly to be the quintessential All American city.

Jim gave the outside of the RV a good bath while I cleaned the inside and Mike supervised. A little boy wearing a "superman" towel cape joined us from across the street to get a better look at the "house on wheels." "You drive your house?" he asked. I invited him inside to have a look. "Cool!" he exclaimed. That night Mike grilled Omaha steaks on the patio and we spent the rest of the evening relaxing and talking about our kids—who just happened to be married to each other and living in Houston, Texas.

The next morning Suzi went to work and Mike was left in charge. First we met all the relatives for a late brunch at a downtown restaurant. Every person we passed seemed to know Mike and after stopping and chatting with each, it took us a while to get inside and seated. Awaiting us at a big table were Mike's sister, aunt and uncle, niece and the family matriarch, 89-year-old Grandma Ethel. I sat next to her and she kept up a sharp conversation about the recent terrorist attacks and what it might mean for the future. She'd lived through plenty of societal upheavals and explained that all the changes the attacks would bring weren't yet obvious. Grandma Ethel was born before her family had electricity and had worked in the family business until she was 85. In discussing her age, she shrugged, "When God comes to tell me it's my time to go, he's going to have a big argument on his hands!"

Mike's niece admitted that she had cancelled a flight to visit Todd and Leslie in Houston that week because ever since 9-11 she'd developed a fear of flying. After seeing the empty airport, I knew she wasn't the only one. Jim said all the planes he'd flown from Greenville had very few passengers. There was much talk as to whether the attacks had made a permanent change in air travel in our country. It had obviously had a terrible effect for the short term.

Following brunch Mike took us to the Omaha Zoo. As a patron he flashed his pass and we walked right through the gates. Again, everyone seemed to know him. We spent the next six hours attempting to take in everything the zoo had to offer—which turned out to be impossible. It was a huge park covering many acres with animals secured in environments that replicated their natural habitat. Overnight the temperature had dropped to the low 30's and it was also windy. We must have walked about ten miles trying to see as much as we could. The Cat Complex and Bear Canyons were especially impressive. But the Nebraska winter had finally arrived and although warmly dressed, we were cold.

The zoo offered electric carts for people with mobility issues and as I was examining one I noticed a small plaque affixed to the frame: *The Charles Mogil Memorial Cart.* Charlie Mogil was Ethel's deceased husband. He immigrated to America from Russia as a young man and his name was listed at Ellis Island as Charles Mogilefsky. Ethel's family, on the other hand, the Rubins, had lived in Omaha since 1850. Their claim to fame is the Rubin sandwich (often misspelled as Rueben). Ethel married Charlie in 1932. During prohibition Charlie ran a speakeasy and tinkered in other enterprises. At various times he owned a grocery store and a bar. During World War II he joined the Navy. When an admiral who had patronized his bar remembered Charlie, he had him moved to his ship and Charlie spent the war as the flagship bartender.

The first Rubins arrived in Omaha when it was still a frontier town. They homesteaded a sheep ranch in Wyoming before moving to the city and entering business. My son-in-law Todd's generation was the first of the Mogil or Rubin families to attend college and enter professional ranks. For many years, Mike Mogil had hosted a huge Fourth of July picnic with hotdogs, hamburgers and fireworks to celebrate the birthday of the nation that had provided his family so many opportunities.

CHAPTER 6

WESTWARD HO

Jim and I waved goodbye to Mike and Suzi the next morning and pointed the Four Winds westward. It was nice to relax in the passenger's seat for a change. Although we'd been advised it was more scenic to the north, we wanted to see more of Nebraska, so headed west across the widest part of the state. Beyond Omaha we began to see open ranges and big sky. It was a land of enormous ranches and crumbling sod houses. We saw lots of cattle grazing, hawks circling and prairie grass extending to the horizon on both sides of the highway.

As we continued westward, Interstate 80 loosely followed the route of the Oregon Trail. There were many historical markers along the way. Although the trail was more than 150 years old, there were places where wheel ruts could still be detected. Tens of thousands of pioneers in Conestoga wagons, on horseback or by foot followed the trail to Wyoming, Idaho, Oregon and California. The trip for those early travelers covered about 2,000 miles through rugged terrain and hostile Indian territory. Without hurrying we planned to take five or six days to cover the same distance that had taken the pioneers five or six months.

For a while we followed the North Platte River that figures so prominently in Old Western lore. The North Platte was once a mile wide as evidenced by the streambed and written records, but the river we followed was about 60 feet across, shallow and slow. It has dwindled due to extensive water diverted for irrigation. In appearance it was a humble river but far from humble in the dramatic history recorded along its banks.

Not only was the highway we traveled near the Oregon Trail, we also came close or crossed over other historical pathways: the Mormon Trail toward Utah and Nevada, the California Trail and the Pony Express. I tried to imagine what it must have been like to journey this way on horseback or in a covered wagon. The landscape was massive and lonely. The trails followed this route because it was flat and treeless and therefore easier on animals and foot-travelers. Also, the rivers were shallow and without swift currents. Still, many people and animals died along these westward tracks.

Without ever leaving Nebraska we put nearly 500 miles on the odometer. Finally, overtired, we checked into an RV park on the outskirts of Scottsbluff, on the state's western edge. The park was adjacent to railroad tracks and much to our annoyance long freight trains rattled by throughout the night. Scottsbluff is a ranching and railroad center for cattle and coal. The smell of cow shit was everywhere.

Although the town is named Scottsbluff, there is also a real Scott's Bluff outside of town. Scott's Bluff is a huge geological spire rising 800 feet above the North Platte River. It can be seen for many miles and served as a landmark to guide the early travelers.

From Scottsbluff we turned north through more of the prairieland that makes up most of Nebraska. The farms and ranches we passed were huge and remote from each other. The land is naturally treeless so most houses had a wind break of carefully planted trees either surrounding or lined along their northern sides. The two-lane highway we traveled was nearly deserted. We passed very few other vehicles.

The late September crop fields were fallow, a muted sage color. The sky was cloudless and pale blue; it seemed to go on forever. It was amazing country. My imagination conjured up a lone Pony Express rider galloping across that rugged, lonely land.

We stopped for lunch at a little café on the main street of Hay Springs, Nebraska, population 652. The special of the day was enchiladas, which turned out to be mountains of chili, cheese, beans, onions and chopped beef. It was authentic "cowboy food" that had more quantity than quality going for it. The restaurant was full of ranchers and one table of dressed up elderly ladies meeting for lunch. We were the only "outsiders" and caught a few curious stares. Before leaving, I purchased a loaf of homemade bread offered for sale at the check-out counter.

We continued driving north and soon entered the Pine Ridge Indian Reservation for the Oglala and Lakota Sioux tribes. The Sioux have one of the more valiant and violent histories of opposition to white incursion. Chiefs Crazy Horse and Sitting Bull were their most renowned leaders. The reservation consisted mostly of scattered small houses, a few bars and liquor stores and several modern "Indian schools." Some of the homes we passed had traditional teepees constructed beside the small siding house or doublewide trailer. The Sioux men we saw wore their hair in long braids or ponytails. We also noticed a number of pinto horses grazing in the fields.

We traveled through the reservation for more than a hundred miles, crossing from Nebraska into South Dakota. The landscape was mostly grassy plains with undulating hills leading to distant mountains. Once in South Dakota we entered the southern edge of the Badlands. This was a rugged, eroded area consisting of gullies and buttes with almost no vegetation. It was once infamous as a hideout for outlaws and renegade Indians. It is also known as a place with huge fossil fields of prehistoric animals. We wanted to see more of the Badlands but the Visitor's Center was closed and we seemed to be the only humans for miles around. So we reluctantly exited the Badlands and headed toward the Black Hills of Dakota.

It was here that we took a side road to visit Wounded Knee. On Dec. 29, 1890, The Battle of Wounded Knee marked the last Indian uprising against the United States and concluded with the conquest of Native Americans. More than 300 Lakota Sioux men, women and children were massacred here by federal soldiers and buried in a mass grave. We had expected some sort of historical marker or monument but instead found only a tiny settlement and modern post office.

We were beginning to wonder if we'd ever reach civilization again when suddenly we came to the outskirts of Rapid City. We noticed an RV Supplies and Repair shop along the highway and stopped to see if they could fix the still-bent back steps. We were the only customers. The owner told us tourist season had ended and yes, he could fix our steps. *Hooray!* It took about 90 minutes and cost only sixty-something dollars. While the steps were being repaired, I purchased, wrote, and mailed postcards.

Not long after leaving the RV shop, we began an ascent into the Black Hills of South Dakota. From the desolate prairie, we had entered a land of rounded hilltops, heavily wooded mountain slopes and deep valleys. The scenery was spectacular in its rugged beauty and was especially affecting after the emptiness of the plains. Each mountain curve we rounded revealed another incredible vista. Around one of these curves we were suddenly presented with the chiseled profile of George Washington against the sky. Mount Rushmore!

We stopped for the night at the Mt. Rushmore KOA with plans to visit the national monument the next morning. Suddenly it occurred to me that on this day I'd been traveling for exactly one month.

Next morning we departed early and headed to Mount Rushmore National Park. Suddenly we saw a mountain goat grazing on the roadside. Jim stopped and I walked back to get as close as I could to take photos. We'd read that the goats were skittish and seldom seen except with binoculars, but this one seemed totally unconcerned that I was across the road snapping his picture. He placidly kept on munching. When finally he looked up and glared, I got a great photograph but decided his expression wasn't friendly, so hurried back to the RV.

Mount Rushmore was astonishing. How one man could conceive, plan and execute such a massive sculpture was hard to imagine. Although two million visitors tour the monument yearly, in late September it was sparsely attended. We first watched a short film about how the sculpture was accomplished. The sculptor Gutzon Borglum carefully planned and plotted, then hired hundreds of local laborers to drill, dynamite and hammer the granite cliff face according to his marks and directions. There were no safe labor laws then and many men were killed or injured in the process. The work began in 1929 and finished in 1941. Borglum chose Washington to represent the founding of America, Jefferson to represent American political philosophy, Lincoln to represent preservation of the union, and Teddy Roosevelt to represent expansion and conservation of the land.

Upon leaving Rushmore, we stopped for a distant look at the equally massive rendition of Chief Crazy Horse on horseback being sculpted into another mountainside. Then we continued exploring the Black Hills. It was slow going on the steep highway. We crossed Harney Pass which at 7242 feet is the highest mountain pass east of the Rockies.

Continuing on, we drove through Hill City, Lead and Deadwood, all old South Dakota mining towns with notorious reputations. Deadwood City was once a center of gambling and prostitution, with many gunfights on its streets. The Number Ten Saloon (still there) is where Wild Bill Hickock was shot in the back by a drunken Jack McCall. Historians claim it was the only time Hickock ever played poker with his back toward the door—he thought it unlucky and dangerous.

We stopped for a wonderful German dinner of wiener schnitzel at Hill City, SD, another mining town. The restaurant was crowded and the food excellent. Then from Hill City we drove to Sturgis, known as the motorcycle capital of America. At this time of year the streets of Sturgis looked sleepy and provincial, but we knew that once a year Sturgis transformed itself into the wildest, rowdiest Main Street in America. More than a half million bikers from all around the world converge on Sturgis for their yearly rally the first week of every August. A shopkeeper told us they'd been doing it almost every year since 1938.

After a long day of sightseeing, we stopped for the night near a little town with the unlikely name of Spearfish, South Dakota. Spearfish, we learned, held the world record for temperature change in the shortest amount of time. On January 22, 1943 at 7:30 AM it was -4 degrees F. Then the Chinook wind blew into town and two minutes later at 7:32 AM it was +45 degrees. In 2001 the record still held. The area was quiet (no Chinooks) and the weather was cold. We were ready for a good night's sleep and turned in early.

The next morning we dipped south into Wyoming and headed for Devil's Tower. Along the highway we saw many prong-horned antelope. Among some of the cattle herds we passed, deer and antelope were grazing side by side with domestic farm animals. Besides deer and antelope, we saw elk, eagles and hawks, and more than a few prairie dog settlements. Wild life was everywhere.

Devil's Tower is a massive natural rock formation created by the solidified lava core of an ancient volcano. It is often recognized as the place where the aliens landed in the movie *Close Encounters of the Third Kind*. As we drove along, there it suddenly was, rising 865 feet into the sky, with fluted sides and a flat top. The circumference at the base is more than a mile.

We listened to a talk by the park ranger then hiked to the base of the big rock. Along the trail were many prayer flags and spirit icons left by Native Americans who consider the spire a holy place. Devil's Tower is closed to outsiders once a year so that Indians can perform religious rituals. The park ranger explained the myth is that the rock tower rose miraculously out of the ground to save four children who were being chased by a giant grizzly. The ridges along the vertical sides are said to be claw marks made by the bear as he tried to get to the children who were safe at the top.

Three mountain climbers were working their way up the west face of the tower, the side considered most difficult to scale. We watched for a while with binoculars. It was a slow and scary ascent that made us jittery just watching.

After leaving Devil's Tower, and stopping to have a look at a massive prairie dog village along the road, we drove through Gillette and Buffalo to Sheridan, Wyoming. The landscape was rolling, lush meadowland. Our destination was Yellowstone National Park but first we had to cross the Big Horn Mountains.

We traversed Granite Pass in the southern Beartooth Range, elevation 9033 feet. The peak towered more than three thousand feet above the pass. The range was named by early explorers who thought the numerous white limestone cliffs looked like bear's teeth. The mountain road was exceedingly steep, sometimes a 12% grade, and Jim often had to gear down the big Chevy engine. There was another road across the pass, one that we didn't take, that was even more scenic but also steeper. The scenery through the Big Horns was more beautiful than anything we'd yet encountered—we realized we are beginning to say that about each new place we visited in that part of the country—but it was true! On one high mountain, we had the new experience of being led through a particularly difficult cliff-side road by a pilot car.

We rushed through Cody to reach the eastern entrance to Yellowstone. Teddy Roosevelt called the road from Cody to the East Gate, "The most beautiful fifty miles in America." We'd heard that traffic could be bumper to bumper at the park during the summer and we didn't know what to expect. There is often snow by late September and Yellowstone was scheduled to close on October 1. We knew none of this before setting out and made it there just in the nick of time. Traffic was minimal yet the weather was perfect, with highs about 70 and nighttime lows about 40 degrees. Everyone told us that the mild weather was unusual. Our visit was perfectly timed although it happened through dumb luck on our part.

Although it was the park's last open weekend until spring, we were able to get into one of the best campgrounds with no reservation. We were one of the last campers admitted but got a beautiful, wooded spot beside Grant Lake. It was dry camping only; no water, electric or sewage hookups are allowed inside Yellowstone.

Just past the East Gate entrance we passed a big male bison wandering along the road. Elk came to drink water across the lake from where we camped, and at night we heard the howling of wolves and coyotes. A big stellar jay perched in the tree next to our picnic table and swooped down to steal any food left unprotected. We kept a close lookout for bears but were told that by late in the season they'd probably gone to higher elevations to gorge in preparation for winter hibernation. We saw no bears.

There was a family with children camped nearby, and since we'd accidentally bought regular caffeine free coke (rather than diet), I took the 12-pack down to offer to them. They were happy to get it. They were a friendly bunch from New Port Richey, Florida. There was Fred and Cheryl with their 29-year-old daughter and five granddaughters all under the age of eight years. All of these people were traveling together in a Lance cab-over pickup camper. Seven females were accompanying Fred as he drove from one end of America to the other buying and selling scrapped fiber optic and telecommunications chips.

The girls, in descending ages from eight to a baby still nursing, were being home schooled by their mother and grandmother. They were extraordinarily beautiful and well-behaved children, with long blond hair and big blue eyes. They told us that their father was an artist who had to remain at home to work. The family invited us to join them around their campfire that evening, a fire Fred kept blazing against the chill night air. The girls chattered and played among the trees, occasionally joining us to warm their hands and roast a marshmallow.

Camping at Grant Lake was our first experience "boondocking"—that is, camping with no hookups. The next morning we set out for Gros Ventre, still in Yellowstone. The park is nearly 3500 square miles in area and 63 miles as the crow flies north to south. The roads wound through forests and meadows and we passed a number of geothermal features, lakes, rivers and waterfalls. There was plenty to see. We soon figured out that when cars are pulled over, wildlife is nearby. At one bend in the road, Jim stopped to see what people were looking at. It was a big moose cow and her calf feeding in the woods. I got close enough to snap several pictures. Later, however, we heard that it probably wasn't such a great idea to get close as mothers can be quite aggressive when they have young.

Although Gros Ventre was advertised as teeming with wildlife, we saw none. Again, we "boondocked" not far from the Gros Ventre River, a beautiful, fast moving stream that looked like the kind of place you might see a grizzly fishing for trout. We saw lots of animal scat and birds but that was all.

After over-nighting at Gros Ventre we headed next toward the Grand Teton Mountains. Some people say these mountains were named by a Frenchman with a sense of humor. As we approached that glorious, mauve, snow-capped range, three voluptuously shaped peaks did rise above the rest (explorers originally called the mountains Les Trois Tetons). We drove through Teton Pass, elevation 8431 feet, toward Jackson Hole. There is no better word for the Grand Tetons than majestic.

At the base of the Tetons, in a wide green valley, was Jackson Hole, Wyoming. I was expecting the old hunting enclave of western lore but what we found was an upscale resort town with lots of pricey shops and restaurants.

From Jackson Hole, we drove through northern Idaho and into southern Montana. The scenery continued to be unendingly magnificent, so much so that "scenic overload" set in. You think that you can't possibly see anything more beautiful and then you do. Wyoming, Idaho and Montana were spectacular. There is nothing in America to compare to the mountains, forests, prairies, gorges, cliffs, valleys, rivers and lakes of those western states.

As September changed to October we drove our longest one-day distance, 528 miles. That's a tiring drive in a motorhome over high mountains. We dipped back into Idaho from Montana and camped beside Lake Coeur d'Alene, a large glacial lake in the Idaho panhandle. The next morning we almost immediately crossed the state line and found ourselves on the outskirts of Spokane, Washington. Once past Spokane, we left behind the scenery. The hills of Idaho suddenly changed to colorless plains with little if any agriculture. Although we knew that Washington was a beautiful state, the eastern part was dry and barren. After more than a hundred miles, we turned south until we reached the Columbia Gorge, formed by the massive Columbia River, which marks the border between Washington and Oregon.

Interstate 84 runs along the Columbia River's southern (Oregon) shore, and State Road 14, a scenic byway, follows the river on its northern (Washington) bank. We decided to take SR 14, of course, and again found ourselves driving through incredible landscape. A narrow flat area contained the roadbed and to the right rose jagged cliffs. Several miles across the water we could see vehicles moving along the Interstate. From our perspective the cars and trucks looked like miniature toys. Historical markers along the way told us that the road we were on was the same path followed by the Lewis and Clark Expedition as they made their way to the Pacific in 1805.

At Vancouver, Washington, we crossed the bridge into Oregon and had a great view of snow-capped Mount Hood in the distance. We hit Portland during rush hour and it took more than an hour to drive from one end of the city to the other. We finally landed at a wonderful RV park in Tualatin, in wine vineyard country southwest of Portland. The park had state-of-the-art hookups at every campsite, including high speed Internet access, so we were able to get online and check e-mail. The weather continued unseasonably warm and the park even allowed guests to wash their rigs (unusual!). We took full advantage.

CHAPTER 7

THE GREAT PACIFIC

Departing the suburban town of Tualatin the next morning, it was a short drive to the Pacific Ocean. Our first sight of the greatest body of water in the world was less than awesome. We turned south onto US 101 and suddenly there it was—not the deep blue breaking waves of expectation but wavelets the color of wet cement lapping a pebbled ochre beach.

For a number of miles we drove past motels and other tourist businesses. It was off season and there were lots of Vacancy signs. A little further along we found ourselves navigating a winding highway that followed the seashore. Deeply forested hills rose to the left of the road and to the right was the ocean. The Pacific finally began to live up to its reputation. The rugged shoreline was spotted with huge boulders, some larger than buildings, and colossal waves crashed against the rocks, spewing up geysers of spray.

The shoreline boulders had been shaped by millenniums of water and climate into countless forms and sizes, some smoothly domed and others jagged and craggy. Bird colonies nested on some of the larger rocks, leaving the tops encrusted with white droppings. From afar, the white-topped rocks looked like snow-capped mountains. The trees near shore were wind sculpted into streamlined silhouettes pointing inland.

The highway continued its gradual ascent, with many twists and turns, but never losing sight of the ocean. We stopped at an overlook with a spectacular view of the pretty red and white Cape Blanco Lighthouse.

That night we camped within sound of the ocean in an RV park that catered to abalone divers. Next morning we woke to the barking of sea lions gathered offshore on rocks. As we drove along, we saw not only the sea lions, but also hundreds of otters cavorting in the surf. We watched as abalone divers in black wetsuits bobbed up and down in the surf, disappearing underwater and then resurfacing like sea mammals.

We knew it was ridiculous but every new place we saw, we proclaimed the best yet. Each new landscape displaced the previous as "most beautiful." As we continued south along the Pacific Coast Scenic Byway, it soon became the redwood forests that took our breath away. The forests of giant conifers were absolutely the most glorious things in nature, we decided. Yes, the Rockies were beautiful, as were the Tetons, and the Oregon coast—but these redwoods took the prize. We hadn't expected it. They were only trees!

We left US 101 to detour on the Newton Drury scenic by-way. (Important road trip rule: always take the roads on the map with the little green dots.) Upon entering the giant redwood forest, it was as if we'd stepped into a cathedral. The trees were more than trees— they were behemoth, grand pillars. The regal architecture of the redwoods literally reached out of sight, with thick, green ferns carpeting the ground beneath, and beams of sunlight darting in laser straight lines through the high branches to the ground. There was an otherworldly, reverential component to the forests. It wasn't a place...it was a *realm*.

We stopped repeatedly to stare at the giants and to get out of the RV and walk among them. All sounds were muffled. It was almost too much to take in. There was a sign leading to "The Big Tree" and we followed the path about 100 yards into the forest to see how "The Big Tree" could possibly be any larger than the rest. The path led to a 304-foot behemoth more than1500 years old. The diameter was 21 feet. Jim and I together with arms outstretched couldn't reach the trunk's curve. A young man walked along with us and he spoke with a Southern accent. He told us that he'd just left his seasonal job at

Yellowstone and was driving in a roundabout way home to Louisiana. When we finally reached "The Big Tree" there was already a young couple there. They spoke with Middle Eastern accents and told us that they were on their honeymoon. All of us took each other's pictures and marveled that Nature had created such a miracle.

After leaving the redwoods we continued on State Route 1 which hugged the mountainous north California shoreline. This is the treacherous two-lane highway sometimes seen in movie chase scenes. Sheer rock cliffs extended upward to the left and downward to the deep blue Pacific Ocean on the right. We traversed many, many bridges along the way.

Finally, we left Hwy 1 to detour 32 miles inland to drive through Humboldt State Park, called "Avenue of the Giants." Here we passed through more unspoiled acres of old growth redwoods. After not seeing them for a while along the coast, one forgets, and then suddenly there you are in another grove of giants; and again we were overwhelmed by their massiveness and the serenity and grandeur of the forest. There is no way to understand what these redwoods are like from looking at pictures. It takes about 400 years for one of these trees to mature and the largest among them were older than double the millennium we were celebrating. You need to actually walk among them to truly comprehend.

Late that morning we came to the hamlet of Redcrest, California, population 89. We stopped at The Shrine Tree Café for breakfast. A young man in his early twenties was the owner, waiter and cook. The menu's specialty was one pancake for $3.75. A bit pricey, we thought, for a single pancake. Don't most restaurants serve three for that amount? Jim ordered it—he wanted to know how they could justify the charge. It turned out to be the best breakfast of the trip, even better than Linda's Café in North Adams, Massachusetts. Jim's pancake came out on a huge platter and that "one pancake" was about 20 inches in diameter and cooked to perfection. It was light and fluffy in the center, brown and crispy on the edges, and served with plenty of real butter and good syrup on the side. A couple of spicy link sausages were sitting on top. I had my usual bacon and eggs with hash-browns which were also cooked to perfection. Jim pronounced the pancake the best he'd ever eaten.

After breakfast we explored the area around the café and found "the shrine tree" for which the café was named. It was the huge trunk of a long dead redwood, hollowed out to form a room of about 12 feet square with an 8-foot ceiling. We went inside and signed the guest book.

A little further down the road we came to the famous "drive-through" tree that appeared on many old post cards. Vehicles could no longer actually drive through the tree unless paying the tree's owner $4.00. I wanted to see it, so we paid and drove through. We learned from the old man selling tickets that the land had been in his family for generations and they had to sell tickets in order to make enough money to pay taxes. It seemed incredible that ordinary people still owned large sections of these national treasure-lands, including, the owner told us, the mineral rights.

Nowadays most redwood forests are publicly owned by the state of California or the U. S. government. There were tasteful signs here and there among the trees that announced, "This grove is maintained by the national park service in memory of so-and-so." I thought that was a great living memorial for someone who loved the redwood forests.

The next day we continued our long drive on steep and winding Highway One. On several occasions we passed areas where the asphalt was eroded on the downhill edge and the road narrowed to one lane. There were often deep drops on the western side of the road, and minimal protective barricades. This would be a horrible drive for someone afraid of heights or bridges. The highway was old, built in the 1920's, and for long stretches there was little or no shoulder. Just cliff, narrow two-lane asphalt road, then another precipice descending hundreds of feet to the Pacific Ocean. It was a driving/riding experience not to be missed but one we didn't want to do again anytime soon—at least not in an RV.

CHAPTER 8

FRISCO AND SOUTHWARD

At mid afternoon we arrived on the outskirts of San Francisco and got our first glimpse of the Golden Gate Bridge. What an awesome sight that was! In the middle of San Francisco Bay was Alcatraz Island and just over the bridge was the Presidio. Almost as soon as we crossed the bridge from the north, we were in downtown San Fran and right on busy Lombard Street.

Suddenly we had an unsettling experience. In front of us was a black Porsche convertible, top down, with two men in it, and to our right was a city bus. Five or six rowdy teenaged boys were hanging waist high out the bus windows, shouting obscenities at passersby. Suddenly they turned their attention to the Porsche and its passengers. The rowdies were shooting the finger, calling the men "faggots" and throwing fruit—not tossing but really line-driving and smashing it against the car. The driver stopped his car, got out and began shouting back, which only fueled the fire. He then jumped back in the Porsche and sped off. The hooligans continued to yell, still hanging out the bus windows. Then one of them noticed our motorhome and hurled a plum that splattered against the windshield. That was hilarious, they thought. It was a very strange welcome to a city often called the most tolerant and sophisticated in America.

We quickly moved ahead of the bus and turned right onto Van Ness Ave. toward the Oakland Bay Bridge. Traffic was backed up and slow moving. It was the first traffic congestion we'd encountered since Portland.

Finally we made our way across the Bay Bridge to Concord and the Sunny Acres Trailer Park. A girl at the desk told us that they could only put us up for two nights in a makeshift spot. We had no choice because nothing else was available. Then when we tried to rent a car, although we'd been assured there would be no problem, we found not one rental was available in all the bay area. Because business had taken such a nosedive after 9-11, the rental agencies were offering super deals as low as $10 a day and there wasn't a single car left on the lots! At least that's what we were told. So we had to unhook and drive the RV to Benihana's Restaurant, where the wedding rehearsal dinner was being held for our niece Laura and her fiancé Rich. We arrived late but at least we got there.

Once settled into "Happy Acres" our bad luck continued. Jim had noticed that the RV's brakes were "soft" as he drove down the coastal highway. We had scheduled ourselves to be in San Francisco when Laura got married, so we stopped at a Midas Muffler Shop to get the brakes checked. The mechanic, however, told us we had a bigger problem than a soft emergency brake. He said that the left brake cylinder was leaking fluid and it was too big a job for him to repair. We needed an authorized Chevrolet truck-van dealership, he said. Meanwhile, he warned that we should not be driving the vehicle.

After making numerous phone calls, we finally got the RV into an authorized dealership in Walnut Creek and they informed us it would take at least two days to do the repairs. Luckily, everything was still under warranty. Unluckily, we had to move to a boring and overpriced motel. No matter, we had a wedding to get to!

The wedding was held outdoors in perfect autumn weather. Before the ceremony, Laura and Rich asked everyone to stand for a minute of silent prayer for the victims of September 11. Since Laura was a flight attendant and Rich a police officer, they asked for special prayers for the many airline personnel and New York policemen and firemen who were killed in the 9-11 terrorist attacks.

The wedding was on October 7. The same day, American planes began bombing in Afghanistan. The morning news announced that all the San Francisco bay bridges were on heightened security alert due to new terrorist threats. Jim had to return to Greenville and he had flight plans from San Francisco. As soon as the brakes were repaired I planned to drive back across the bridges to Novato, where my friend Robin lived.

We were stuck in the motel and there was still constant news about the attacks and America's response. In Florida a man had died from a very rare case of anthrax. Several other cases had popped up in the northeast. Suspicion was growing that America might also be under a biological germ attack. President Bush had started an undeclared war against "terrorists" in Afghanistan and people were receiving anthrax germs through the mail. The news was one frightening story after another. Meanwhile Osama bin Laden had released videotape threats that played incessantly on television. In it he declared that the US would not have peace until peace reigned in Palestine. He called Americans "infidel devils" and praised the "martyrs" who flew the planes into the Twin Towers and Pentagon.

Everything seemed to be changing. There was lots of conjecture about what might come next but very few hard facts to back anything up. Airline travel—travel in general—had plummeted since 9-11. I felt fortunate that I'd begun my trip prior to that terrible day. Otherwise, I probably wouldn't have set out. Yet I did and I'd seen the Twin towers in their last days. My trip had become a ringside seat as the U. S. adapted to a strange and harsh new reality. This was always in the background as I journeyed across the incredible beauty of the American land.

Jim left the next morning. The Chevrolet mechanic had discovered that both rear axle seals were leaking fluid and the brake shoes were soaked. We had luckily escaped what could have been a disaster as we drove over the mountains and down rugged Highway One. The whole brake system had to be replaced, a big and expensive job that should have been caught and fixed when we originally complained about soft brakes to the RV dealer when we purchased the Four Winds.

It wasn't easy for Jim to get to the airport. First he took the motel shuttle to BART (Bay Area Rapid Transit), and then rode BART to its last stop. He next caught another shuttle to San

Francisco International Airport. Difficulty was increased because BART and the airport were both under tight security that required extra screening. Jim went through three metal detectors and three open bag searches before he was finally allowed to board his flight to Atlanta.

I had to check out of the motel by noon and was left with five hours to kill before the RV would be ready. I spent the afternoon walking around and exploring Walnut Creek. It was an appealing little town with lots of shops and restaurants along Main and Locust Streets. There was a small restaurant called the Afghanistan Café. I passed it at lunchtime and looked through the big front windows to see tables set up with spotless white napery and vases of greenery. Although all other restaurants in the area were packed, the Afghanistan Café didn't have a single customer. They'd put a big American flag in the window and a sign proclaiming "God Bless America." Seeing that empty cafe with its patriotic sign was a sad commentary on how the terrorists had wounded commerce and relationships in this country.

Finally, I made my way to the Walnut Hills Mall. I was walking through Nordstrom's when my cell phone rang. My friend Becky was calling to tell me that her boyfriend Bill's cancer had spread to his bones. A non-smoker, he'd been diagnosed with lung cancer only three months before. Bill believed his cancer was caused by the Agent Orange he'd been repeatedly exposed to in Vietnam. She said that Bill was doing chemo and seemed to be handling it well. "He's young, he can beat it," Becky insisted. We made plans for me to visit them in Georgia before I returned home.

The RV was ready to go at five that afternoon. It wasn't the best time to be setting out on San Francisco freeways but I had no choice. In an attempt to avoid the worst traffic, I decided to go around the top of the bay rather than back through the middle of town. My plan was futile; the traffic was terrible and it took almost three hours to reach Robin's house in Novato.

Earlier in the afternoon I'd gotten my hair cut at a walk-in salon and the hairdresser had cut it too short. I tried to comb it this way and that in an attempt to make it look better but it was hopeless. I was in a foul humor. Showing up at Robin's house with bad hair and a sour mood was not what I'd planned. Although we'd kept in touch, I hadn't actually seen my friend in more than thirty years. In my mind we were still the two crazy kids who had once roomed together in the French Quarter in New Orleans. The woman who came running out of the house had the same sparkly eyes, the same chirpy voice and the same long, brown hair. But this Robin was...*older*. We looked quizzically at each other, then suddenly the years peeled away and we embraced in an exuberant hug. Thirty-something years disappeared in a poof!

Robin's son Darren hooked the RV to their electricity with a long cable to the garage, and that's where I slept for the next several nights—parked on a residential street in Novato. The house where Robin and Darren lived was a "fixer-upper" they'd recently purchased and were in the process of renovating. The guest bedroom was packed with building materials and was temporarily unusable. They said they'd paid $345,000 for the little house with no air conditioning, no working heat, and the garage roof falling in. It was a project like Robin and Darren had done repeatedly. They purchased run-down property in good locations, lived in it while renovating, then sold at a nice profit. The San Francisco housing market was booming.

Robin also owned and operated an art gallery in Port Reyes. While she worked at the gallery each day, Darren worked on the house. He had his contractor's license and was a master electrician. The house was a simple 1200 square feet, three-bedrooms, one-bath tract home built just after World War II. It had probably cost the original owners about $12,000. Darren was in the middle of knocking out walls, re-wiring, putting in new floors, a new fireplace, raising the ceilings and painting everything inside and out. They'd already installed big new windows and built a brick patio across the back. "We could sell it right now for $450,000 but it will be worth even more when we finish," Robin said. I couldn't believe it. Welcome to Marin County real estate circa 2001!

I was happy to be in my own small space again. The previous several weeks of sharing with Jim, then the wedding weekend followed by the mechanical difficulties and repairs, had been tiring. I could hardly wait to get comfy in my cab-over loft and return to reading *The Blind Assassin*. During the day, Robin and I visited, and at night I had my own space to do as I pleased.

The day after I arrived, Robin took me to her gallery at Point Reyes Station. It was a beautiful 20-mile drive through rolling hills. Point Reyes Station was an old California seaside village that attracted "arty" types from San Francisco and Sacramento. Darren and Robin had first searched for a "fixer-upper" home there but soon discovered that no one of normal income could afford the prices. The most modest bungalows cost $700,000 and up, Robin said. That left locals as only the very wealthy or those who had lived in Port Reyes for many years. She said it was slowly becoming a town of Bed and Breakfasts, galleries and restaurants. After looking for real estate in Point Reyes Station, Novato seemed reasonable in comparison.

Robin was a painter known in California art circles for her impressionist plein aire landscapes. Several years before she had purchased The William Lester Gallery, a long established Point Reyes business. In the first year she was able to increase sales by 64%. But since 9-11 business had drastically fallen off. It was yet another example of how the terrorist attacks were effecting American lives in a harmful manner.

Robin and I walked along the nearby Point Reyes National Seashore. We talked about our first meeting in New Orleans and how we'd instantly hit it off. I had met our mutual friend Mike (then a student at Tulane) on one of my flights, and for some now-forgotten reason had revealed to him my unsatisfactory living arrangements (five girls in a two bedroom apartment in Metairie). "I know someone you need to room with," he told me. "Trust me, you'll love her." The next day he took me to Robin's lodging in a house in the Garden District. She wasn't home—Mike had neglected to inform her he was bringing over a potential roommate. I wanted to leave but Mike insisted we wait till she returned.

After a while the trolley came clanging down St. Charles Avenue and stopped at the corner of Jefferson Street. Off the trolley hopped a slender girl with long, gold-brown hair flying in the breeze, her face obscured behind the huge potted fern she was carrying. Robin had taken the trolley downtown to purchase a houseplant at

Woolworth's. And Mike was right; we became instant best friends as only the very young and unsuspicious can. She was from Maine; I was from Alabama. She was teaching 5th grade at a Catholic school; I was a stewardess for a regional airline. We were both trying to become artists. We quickly found a furnished fourth-floor walk-up attic apartment on the corner of Royal and St. Philip Streets in the French Quarter. It had a slanted ceiling, two dormer windows and one original brick wall. The monthly rent was a whopping $365— pretty steep we thought. It was in a 300-year-old building which that year had won a historical restoration award. Neither one of us could really afford our half of the rent but that didn't matter. We lied about our incomes to the manager and moved right in.

After exploring the magnificent Port Reyes National Seashore, Robin treated me to lunch at a Cal-Mex restaurant near the gallery. I had yummy chicken mole and Robin feasted on fish tacos. Then we returned to Novato and I retired happily into my snug little camper. No television, no worrisome war reports, no dinner to cook, no chores, no phone calls. I'd lost track of what was happening in Afghanistan. I knew I'd learn soon enough. For the moment, all I wanted to do was forget about trouble, read, write in my journal and live day by day. I hadn't seen a newspaper in weeks. It was good to be distracted from the national anxiety. I had finally weaned myself from being fixated on the daily news.

Next morning I woke early and decided it was time to get moving again. The early hour gave me plenty of time to get the RV unhooked, battened down and ready to roll before Robin showed up for coffee. It was another few hours before I actually pulled out. Once Robin and I started talking, time disappeared. There were so many shared memories of our life in New Orleans. One memory led to another and we laughed a lot.

By 10:30 AM I was again crossing the Golden Gate Bridge. I'd heard on the radio that due to new terrorist threats security was at peak level and traffic was predicted to be light. Instead, I found the bridge swarming with people and vehicles. In fact, it was busier than when Jim and I had first crossed. It seemed as if the people of San Francisco were out in force with an "in your face" attitude. There were cars, trucks, motorcycles and bicycles, pedestrian traffic and skaters. I even saw a few young skateboarders. People seemed especially jovial, laughing and calling to each other, and I saw more than a few flags. I thought, well, if we get blown up today we'll all go down with a defiant attitude. I loved seeing how the people of San Francisco were reacting to the latest terrorist intimidation.

I was so distracted by all the activity that I missed moving into the wide aisle at the toll plaza. Suddenly my side mirror was firmly wedged against a pole in the general traffic lane. I couldn't move either forward or backward. Instead of being helpful, the toll taker suddenly looked right at me and screamed, "Some people were put on this earth to make my life hell!" At first I thought he was joking, but no—he continued to glare and angrily mutter, his face getting redder by the second. I didn't know what to do. I started to apologize but he was having none of it. "Get moving! Get moving!" he screamed.

I was stuck hard, my mirror firmly wedged, unable to back up due to the now honking cars behind me, and I couldn't open the door to reach and fold the mirror in against the chassis. I was afraid if I forced my way forward, both mirrors would break off. Then suddenly an angel appeared, the female toll taker from the next isle left her booth to run over and fold both my mirrors in so that I could squeeze through and proceed. She meanwhile gave the apoplectic toll taker who was still shouting a nasty look which I thoroughly appreciated. He could have done what she did a lot easier. I wanted to thank her but had to move on as quickly as possible. I'd been through many toll booths but had never encountered one not wide enough to accommodate the full width of my vehicle's extended mirrors. Now I learned the hard way that there was good reason for the wide aisle at some toll plazas.

With mirrors folded in and unable to unfold them, I was driving blind as to cars behind or to the side. Traffic was brisk. As I crept along, vehicles zipped around me on both sides, some honking their annoyance at my slow speed. My heart was thumping. *What to do?* With fingers crossed and blinkers blinking, I very slowly and carefully inched my way to the far right lane and finally into a parking lot. It was a huge relief to unfold and readjust the mirrors so that I could once again see what was behind and to the side of my RV.

After driving through downtown San Francisco, and through the seemingly endless suburbs south of the city, I finally reached state road 156 to the coast. The scenery immediately changed from asphalt and commerce to lovely seaside vistas. I drove through Monterrey and Carmel and then Big Sur, which I promptly decided was second only in California-style beauty to the Redwood forests. The Big Sur consisted of heavily wooded mountains, cliffs and sweeping hillsides that led down from the two-lane road to the turbulent, deep blue Pacific.

Since it was Saturday, I began searching early for a place to stay the night. I lucked into one of the last spots at the Big Sur Campground and parked under a magnificent redwood. The redwoods were so thick in camp that they blocked out the sun. Everything was shade. I was looking forward to turning in early when at 8 PM music began blaring through the trees. Just across the creek, no more than 100 feet from where I thought I'd been fortunate to park, a boisterous group was dancing to a live rock band. There was lots of hootin', hollerin' and partying going on. With signs posted all around the camp that said, "No loud noise after 8 PM"—they had nevertheless rented the area to a wedding party. I walked to the office to voice a complaint and found myself in the back of a line.

My young next door neighbors walked over and introduced themselves as Kurt and Tressa from Austria. They had flown to Los Angeles and rented a small RV to see "the real America." I wanted to tell them that what they were seeing in California wasn't exactly "real America," but held my tongue. It was as real as anywhere else. I'd seen plenty of differences in America but all were equally "real." It brought home to me again what a varied and vast country we have.

The raucous music finally stopped about ten, followed by the revelers loudly protesting from across the creek. They were shouting that the band was hired to play till midnight. I guess the camp managers finally had to act upon all the complaints they were getting from disgruntled campers who did not come to a redwood grove in the Big Sur to listen to *I Love Rock and Roll*.

For two days I drove at a leisurely pace and stopped early, in no hurry to get anywhere. From a distance, I saw the Hearst Castle at San Simeon but decided not to take the $14 tour. At the town of Cambria, I turned east onto Hwy 46, which I soon discovered was another tour to feast the eyes. I meandered through dun-colored hills, sparsely populated with ranches and vineyards. At one spot I stopped and took photographs of clouds blanketing the San Joaquin Valley below the road.

That night I stopped in the cowboy and wine vineyard town of Paso Robles. After watching 60 Minutes on television, I went to bed and began reading *The Blind Assassin* but soon began to nod off. By nine I was asleep.

CHAPTER 9

INSIDE CALIFORNIA

Having gone to sleep early, I was up early as well at 4:30 AM. It was an unusual schedule for me. I finally figured out that my body clock was stuck three hours ahead on Eastern Time. As soon as it would have been 9 AM in Greenville, I telephoned the office secretary to touch bases and catch up on work info. She told me that business had dropped off significantly since 9-11. She dropped the bombshell that my boss was seriously thinking about shutting down the business. This information was shocking. Before leaving, I'd joked that I might not have a job when I returned but I didn't believe it. Dan needed me too much—or so I thought. We'd had as much business as we could handle. Now suddenly the future looked uncertain. Jim was still looking for a job and I might be out of one as well. Nevertheless, all that seemed far removed from my life at the moment. *I'll think about it when I get home,* I thought. That had become my default mental mantra when considering the future.

Leaving Paso Robles, I passed many elegant haciendas surrounded by grapevines neatly spread on wooden frames. I wanted to stop and take pictures but there was nowhere to pull over. Beyond the vineyards and wineries were almond farms. At some point I crossed the San Andreas Fault. Then suddenly the land became flat again and turned into brown desert studded with huge electrical towers and oil wells. There were refineries and other industrial structures in the distance. The closer I got to Bakersfield, the more industrial the landscape became.

I stopped at an in-town, crowded RV park and got one of the last available spaces. I was directed to the far back of the park and had to back into the tightest squeeze I'd yet encountered. The old man parked next to my site watched skeptically as I expertly guided my Four Winds backward onto the narrow concrete pad that backed up to a tall, woven metal fence. I didn't make a single wrong move and was relieved to pull it off without a hitch, especially since I had an audience. I'd come a long way since initial nervousness at driving such an awkward vehicle. My skills had improved with practice.

The reason I stopped at that particular park was because they advertised that every campsite had an Internet hook-up. Also, they provided cable television connections. I felt I'd ignored the news for long enough. I'd lost track of what was happening in Afghanistan or with the anthrax scare. Although the terrorist attacks were more than a month past, the news was still full of those events.

I'd never seen so much patriotism displayed. A number of the cars and trucks I saw on the California highways had some sort of American flag attached. Every pedestrian overpass that I passed on the Los Angeles freeways had homemade signs hanging from them proclaiming God Bless America or United We Stand. Apparently, Osama Bin Laden had managed to accomplish what no American leader had been able to do in a long time, that is to bring all the different and contentious factions in the country together in one seemingly solid and united front.

The regulation sheet handed out at check-in said Quiet time was 9 PM to 8 AM. Sounded good to me; I was sleepy after waking so early that morning. At 10 PM I was sound asleep when the first train rumbled by, jolting me awake. Every 10 to 15 minutes thereafter, another train thundered past, often with its horn blasting. Sometimes there seemed to be multiple trains passing in both directions and the clamor was deafening. I should have suspected something because of the high privacy fence at the rear of my campsite.

I had never heard such loud noise. But then I'd never "slept" (if you can call it that) so close to trains, either. I had always loved the sound of trains—from a distance! But that night it sounded as if they were about to crash right into my camper. And when they weren't screeching past, I heard the metallic grind and scrape of tracks being switched. I hadn't thought to bring earplugs. There was also heavy truck traffic on a nearby highway overpass. The trucks alone would have been annoying, but add the trains and the sound level was intolerable. I closed all the windows, covered my head with pillows and stuffed Kleenex in my ears. Nothing worked to drown out the cacophony. The RV literally shook from the clamor. It was maddening! I hardly slept at all. Finally, I gave up, turned on the light and tried to read; but that was impossible, too.

About daybreak, I heard the old couple next door unhooking their trailer and leaving. They were grumbling about the train noise, as tired and angry as I was. I went outside and peeked through a gap in the privacy fence. Stretching as far as could see was a huge rail yard with multiple tracks and warehouses. The first track was not far at all from the thin metal barricade my RV was nosed up to.

Since I'd been on the Blue Ridge Parkway in late August, I'd encountered almost no rain; record heat had accompanied me everywhere. In cooler climes that was fine. Seventy degrees in Yellowstone was perfect. But that morning in Bakersfield it was HOT. It was 99 degrees and I still had to get cleaned up, unhooked, and on to my friend Sybil's house. Since the sun came up, the trains had disappeared. Loud noises all night long but none during the daylight--it was weird.

Finally with the welcome quiet, I relaxed in the air conditioning, made a few phone calls and planned my day. I was aware what a strange interlude it was in my life. I was traveling across America while seeing the most amazing sights and having new experiences. In a time of turmoil, my own life had become simpler and more tranquil. I reflected on this as I wrote in my journal. My journey had provided a buffer zone that even a night of enervating train noise couldn't remove me from.

Before going to Sybil's house, I stopped at a Bakersfield truck stop and got in line for a wash. There my little Four Winds was lined up between two 18-wheelers, and although I thought of my vehicle as large, she was really only a little longer than the giant trucks' cabs. The truck stop charged $25 for a wash and they did a fantastic job, even cleaning the engine. My Four Winds came out looking brand new.

While I was waiting a big, fancy truck was being washed in the next bay area. The tall, black driver nodded hello and gave me a quizzical look. I'd gotten used to occasional curiosity of people not used to seeing a lone woman driving a rig. The man asked where I was traveling. "From South Carolina all over the country," I answered. "You're kidding," he said. Then he asked, "Where in South Carolina?" and I answered, "Greenville." A huge smile suddenly crossed his face. "I live between Greenville and Columbia," he said. "Small world!" So then of course we had a nice chat about how far from home we both were and what a coincidence it was to be in the same Bakersfield, California truck wash at the same time.

By 1 PM I was parked in Sybil's driveway. She'd lived in the same house for 40 years. It was a lovely, established neighborhood and she made me feel welcome and comfortable. For a few days, I could get out of the RV and sleep in a real bed.

Sybil was an amazing woman who lived a remarkable life. As she put it, "I'm knocking on 80's door." That September she would reach her eightieth birthday but you'd never know it by her looks or actions. She maintained many friendships of all ages and her telephone rang constantly. She walked daily for several miles, played golf, volunteered at several organizations, traveled, and served as the only female board member of the International Golf Collector's Society. That was where she and I had first met. Sybil had one of the most extensive collections of women's golf memorabilia in the world. Actually, she had one of the best collections of golf antiquities, period.

She had come to Bakersfield when she got her first teaching job at Bakersfield High School. Eventually she taught at Bakersfield College and for 25 years served as an athletic coach there. When she was in her twenties, Sybil took mountaineering lessons in Switzerland, and over her lifetime had climbed many of the world's most challenging peaks. She continued climbing mountains until she was in her early 70's, but after two falls in which she was saved only by safety ropes, she finally decided it was time to give up that particular activity.

Sybil was married several times but never had children. She still got plenty of attention from men, one of them an active nonagenarian. She was an orphan who'd been raised in a Colorado mining town and moved to Bakersfield right out of college. She had always taken great pride and been involved in her community.

For lunch she took me to a Basque restaurant (Bakersfield was originally settled by Spanish sheepherders). It was a homey, unpretentious place with rows of multi-generational family photos lining the walls and a loud and enthusiastic crowd of regulars. We waited to be seated longer than was necessary because Sybil insisted we be in the area of her special longtime server, Jeanette. Sybil said to her, "Take care of us, Jeanette," and Jeanette answered, "You know that I will." Then the wiry, energetic waitress immediately began a parade presentation of the day's selection of Basque specialties. The food was served "family style" from steaming bowls placed in the center of the table. There were potatoes, onions and cabbage, a big bowl of salad greens, beans, lamb, and a rich and flavorful oxtail stew. Warm, crusty bread was served on the side. The food was hot, hardy and delectable.

After lunch Sybil took me on The Grand Tour of Bakersfield in her Cadillac. We went to Gold House, a restored mansion located downtown where she did volunteer work. We also visited Dewar's, a candy company in business since 1942. At Dewar's, Sybil sneaked and bought a two-pound box of their signature taffy chews all for me. Delicious! I continued to enjoy that peanut butter and almond flavored candy for the rest of my trip.

We also visited Sybil's friend, a young German engineer named Gaby. Gaby and her American husband were building a cabin on a mountain near the Sequoia National Forest, land that Sybil either gave or sold or let them use—I never quite understood the arrangement. That's the sort of generosity Sybil was known for. She invited me to visit the cabin with her so that we could hike among the sequoias. It would just be for a night or two. But stupid me, I turned her down. I felt that I'd already overstayed and needed to be on my way. It was a decision I later regretted.

Before I left, Sybil gave me a wonderful gift. As a young teenager, while staying with relatives in Los Angeles, she heard from someone who worked at the airport that there was a chance Amelia Earhart might fly in the next day. Next morning Sybil borrowed a brownie camera and rode the bus to the airport. She waited patiently all day. Then sure enough, late in the afternoon with only Sybil to greet her, Amelia's biplane swooped out of the clouds and taxied to a private hangar. Sybil chased across the tarmac. Amelia was tired, disheveled and carrying a stack of newspapers when she finally emerged from the hangar. Sybil asked if she could take her picture and Amelia replied, "Sure, kid, but only if you promise not to tell anyone I'm in town." Sybil promised, snapped a picture, and kept her mouth shut. Before I left Bakersfield, Sybil presented me with a copy of that still unpublished 1930's photograph.

Departing Bakersfield, Santa Paula was my destination. I crossed the Sierra Madres, yet another impressive mountain range, undulating and amber in color, nothing like the blue-green ridges of the East or craggy snow-capped peaks of the Northwest. Beyond the mountains orange groves stretched as far as the eye could see and migrant farm workers were scattered among the trees on ladders harvesting the crop. I stopped at a roadside stand and bought a 15-pound bag of just picked Valencia's. They were as big as softballs, plump and juicy and easy to peel. I gorged on them. I ate about four before making myself stop.

When I reached the campground at Santa Paula, I was out of luck. It was full of "snowbirds" just arrived for the winter. "This time of year the Canadians flock in like geese," the proprietor said. So on I drove, hoping to make it through Los Angeles before stopping for the night. First, however, I pulled into a mall parking lot to stretch my legs and have a look around Ventura, an upscale beach community just north of LA.

I spent less than an hour walking around and having a cup of coffee at Starbucks. Ventura was nice but I needed to get back on the road before the afternoon traffic rush. On the edge of Los Angeles, I stopped to fill the gas tank and suddenly saw gasoline gushing from beneath the RV's chassis. As fast as I was putting it in, the gas was pouring onto the concrete. A man at the station looked underneath and told me the filler hose had a gaping slit in it. He nonchalantly said they'd been seeing a lot of such vandalism. Someone would crawl and hide under big vehicles, he said, then cut the fuel hose to siphon out the gas. How this could have happened in broad daylight in a busy parking area made no sense to me. "They don't care," the man said. "Damn thieves put little children up to it. They slide under your vehicle and nobody sees anything." This had become particularly problematic since gasoline had hit more than $2 a gallon. The man told me I needed to get to a "real" service station that did repairs, and he directed me to the nearest one.

When I finally inched my way through heavy street traffic to the "real" service station I could find no one there who spoke English. Finally, a Mexican attendant brought over a Vietnamese mechanic and pointed toward his mouth. "He spik englaise," he explained. The young Vietnamese, who appeared to be about seventeen years old, looked at my gas line and shook his head. "Can't fix," he said. "You need Chevy dealer. Have duct tape? You fix!"

Trying to control growing exasperation and anger, not to mention dread and despair, I moved the RV to a gravel lot behind the station. My gas tank was nearly empty and I was stuck somewhere in sprawling LA. Pretending I knew what I was doing, I got on my back and slid under the chassis. The foot-long slit in the fuel hose was easy enough to see. I struggled to wrap multiple layers of silver duct tape around the hole. "You get that fix soon, tape not last," the mechanic shouted at me from where he was working on someone else's car.

A man waiting for his car noticed my efforts and walked over. At least he could speak English. "You aren't planning to drive across LA now, are you?" he asked in a slow drawl. "Well...yes...I was." "Don't even think about it," he advised. "At this time of day it will take you four or five hours and that tape might not hold. If I was you I'd turn around and go back north and find somewhere to stop. Then I'd see about getting that properly taken care of before trying to travel." I was grateful for the advice and thanked him profusely.

That's why I backtracked to Ventura and hooked up in a resort campground that catered to vacationing families. It was the first place I came to. There was no water, no sewage (not even a dump station), and no television connection. It cost about twice what I was used to paying but I was glad to be there. It was across the street from the beach and I was able to open all the windows, feel a nice breeze and listen to the ocean.

The woman who checked me in at the Ventura Park was about forty years old, petite, blond and physically fit. She asked if I were traveling alone and I told her I was. "Me, too," she exclaimed, "and I'm having the time of my life!" She explained that she was working temporarily at the camp to pay for her space and make a few extra bucks. "Once you get settled I'd love to hear your story." At any other time I would have been friendlier; I would have loved to talk to her and swap road tales, but on that day, with all that had happened, I was just too stressed and wiped out to want to talk to anyone.

Next morning I hit the floor running. I was up at dawn to find somewhere to get my fuel hose repaired. This involved first making numerous phone calls to various insurance hotlines and getting put on hold at each. At least it was three hours later in the East and businesses were already open. The Chevy people were as helpful as could be and got me in with a dealership in Oxnard, only one suburb south of Ventura. The people in Oxnard were exceedingly accommodating also and agreed to replace the entire assembly even though it was probably damaged by vandalism. The Four Winds was still under warranty. All I had to do was have the vehicle there before 8 AM.

Somehow I made it. It would take six to eight hours to fix, they told me. Okay, I didn't care. They had a nice waiting room with a coffee machine and magazines. I met a congenial woman who was also waiting and she invited me to accompany her home in the shuttle so that I wouldn't have to spend all day sitting in a sterile waiting room. She assured me that she was a housewife with three kids and not an ax murderer, but I appreciatively declined. She insisted I take her email address and keep her informed about the rest of my trip. She really was a very nice woman and I would have liked to email her except that I lost her address.

Rather than sitting in the waiting room for the entire time, I finally left and began walking. I had no idea where I was or where I was going. I trudged about a mile to a shopping area and then walked back. The whole way was along a busy thoroughfare and I breathed in lots of noxious fumes. The only humans I encountered not in cars were some kids on bicycles and a ragtag man and woman on foot. I nodded hello, as did they. Then the man asked me if I had any money "for food." I hated that! I hated to say no but shook my head. He shrugged, let it go and said, "Thanks anyway."

By the time I returned to Tobey Chevrolet I was dripping with sweat and my lungs felt bruised. What a relief to see my gleaming Four Winds parked in front and ready to go. I had a completely new fuel delivery apparatus and it didn't cost me a cent.

It was mid-afternoon when I finally set out to cross the Los Angeles metropolis. I had already made up my mind to go through the middle of it rather than take a bypass, no matter what. Ever since traveling I-95 through New York I'd stuck with my plan to take the most direct route through cities and I wasn't about to stop now. Seeing downtown was always more interesting than passing by the indistinguishable strip malls and fast food emporiums that populated city outskirts. LA traffic was congested but not horrible. To pass the time I listened to the radio. Between rehashes of Nine Eleven news, there were many announcements of locations that motorists should avoid. Also, flashing overhead signs told where traffic was slow or backed up. Since I didn't know my way around, I plowed ahead trusting dumb luck. Radio announcers also requested various translation volunteers. For instance, "The LAPD needs someone to translate Korean and Spanish at such and such intersection." Or, "sheriff's deputies at this and that street need a volunteer who speaks Russian."

I decided to relax, put on some music and ignore the traffic. Good plan! It ended up taking me more than three hours to traverse the 107 miles from Oxnard until the urban sprawl finally trickled out south of LA. I took 101 to 405 to 5, etc. This route led through Thousand Oaks, Beverly Hills, Hollywood, Santa Monica, Long Beach and Irvine. The worst traffic was on the Santa Monica Freeway. Everything got really clogged around Beverly Hills but I didn't mind because it gave me opportunity to rubberneck. I kept hoping that I'd see a movie star. I certainly saw plenty of BMWs and Mercedes but couldn't see beyond their dark tinted windows. There was one very handsome guy in a BMW convertible just ahead of me but all I could think was how unhealthy it was to be driving in the hot sun while breathing those freeway fumes.

Being in no hurry, I motioned cars with their turn signals on to pull around and in front of me. A few drivers gave me looks as if I were completely nuts. Shades of New York! Memories flooded back of my white-knuckle trip across the George Washington Bridge when no one would let me into the left lane. Smog, traffic, urban sprawl and aggressive drivers—I decided Los Angeles made New York seem almost polite in comparison. In New York no one would make eye contact but in LA they locked eyes and glared.

That night I made it to Oceanside on highway 1 between Los Angeles and San Diego. Oceanside appeared to be a past-its-prime tourist town which hadn't quite yet evolved into quaintness. As it was, the place where I landed was clean and cheap...and lowbrow enough to appeal to my sense of the funky. Best of all, it was near the Pacific Ocean. I decided to stay for several days to recuperate from my LA experience. The *piece de resistance* was that my campsite came decorated with a hand-painted concrete gnome and toadstool. Oh, my, yes—tacky-shabby-trailer-park-chic!

That night I finally had time to catch up with what was happening in the rest of the world. Television news was still full of the anthrax scare. Congress had admonished everyone to live life as usual but when an anthrax-laced letter turned up in Speaker of the House Tom Dashiell's office, Congress immediately adjourned. Much more anthrax had shown up in post offices than in the Halls of Congress but of course postal workers couldn't adjourn and go home. Congress could and they did.

CHAPTER 10

SO CAL

I reluctantly departed Oceanside to continue on coastal highway 101 the sixty or so miles further south to San Diego. The road was choked with traffic and led through a string of small seaside towns. At Leucadia, proceeding at no more than 25 mph, my right side mirror suddenly crashed into the left side mirror of a gleaming new Ford F-250 pickup truck parked at the curb. My mirror folded in but the one on the truck snapped backward and shattered. I couldn't avert the collision because of the narrowness of the road, the extension of both mirrors, and the fact that cars were bumper to bumper on both my lane and the one to my left. Swerving was impossible. Mirror tip to mirror tip, my Four Winds was ten feet wide. The F-250 was a big, wide truck with its own outstretched mirrors. The accident was unavoidable.

A bunch of Hispanic men came spilling out of the tavern the truck was parked in front of. I heard angry shouting in Spanish but couldn't stop due to the ongoing traffic. As soon as I reached a side street I turned around and returned to the scene of the crime. I pulled into a nearby park and walked back to where all the men were now gathered around the brand new truck with its broken mirror. They were shocked that I'd returned and talked rapidly in Spanish.

I felt terrible and apologized to the owner. He walked back with me to the park, his friends following about 15 feet behind, no doubt ready to give chase in case I tried to run. I gave him all my insurance information and called State Farm, but because it was Sunday, all I could do was report the accident to the regional office in Atlanta. They said they would take care of repairing Mr. Rosales' mirror and that all he had to do was take his truck to an authorized Ford dealer as soon as possible. The mirror would be replaced with a new one.

Mr. Rosales didn't seem to believe that my insurance would actually pay. He told me in heavily accented English that if I'd just give him $100 now, he'd let me go. But finally the insurance adjuster in Atlanta convinced him that his truck would be made good as new—and it was a repair job that would cost a good deal more than $100. Nevertheless, he insisted upon writing down every bit of information he could think to ask me. By the time we finished our long discussion and information swap, he finally relaxed and thanked me for stopping and returning to the scene. He said he'd had the truck only for a few days and it was his pride and joy. We shook hands three or four times and his nearby compadres finally saw that everything was okay. They smiled, waved and returned to the tavern.

The mirror crash was a lesson for both of us. I figured Mr. Rosales would probably think twice before parking again on busy Hwy 101, Leucadia, and I learned that in future it would be best that I avoid busy narrow roads with parallel parking alongside. It was an expensive lesson.

That night I pulled in to a bucolic RV park east of San Diego near El Cajon. I first drove through the city and even got off the freeway to have a look at San Diego State College where my friend Laurie was a teacher. My plan was to see Laurie while there, but first I wanted a few days to myself. I had planned to get some writing done in Oceanside but got lazy and ended up spending more time reading, watching TV and wandering on the beach than sitting at the computer. The El Cajon location seemed more amenable to working.

I was conscious of what a rare opportunity I had. When my journey began in late August 2001, the timing had been incredibly serendipitous. I'd had a ringside seat to observe America before and after what everyone was calling Nine Eleven. I was continuing to see the most remarkable effects resulting from that catastrophe. It would always be a pivotal date in American history and I had observed the reaction of people and places from my ever-changing, cross-country vantage point. It was a momentous, reflective time and I wanted to write everything down while it was still fresh in my mind.

I had landed at Rancho Los Coches, a campground located on an old California ranch. There was a windmill house on a hill overlooking the park and a nice walking trail that led across a creek onto boulders that had circular indentations worn by Indian women grinding grain for hundreds of years. The park was partially barricaded by a field of cacti that the park brochure explained had been planted by early ranchers as a natural defense against predators, both animal and human. The park felt safe and almost rural.

I hadn't yet seen Laurie although we talked on the telephone. When I first got to San Diego she was leaving the next morning for a conference in Mexico City. She returned several days later and had to teach a class in the border town of Calexico. Then the day after that she had teaching duties at San Diego State. Plus, she was in charge of a union "teach in" at the college. I couldn't have picked a more inopportune time to show up.

Laurie's absence gave me some "found" time, however, that I used to accomplish three good days of writing. Each morning I ate a small breakfast, then made telephone calls and wrote postcards. After that I did what chores needed to be done, such as laundry and cleaning. It was quick work. The RV was small enough to easily keep everything tidy and organized. If I didn't, the mess quickly got out of hand. It was much like living on a 22-foot boat.

After everything was shipshape, I booted up my laptop and wrote. It was usually difficult to begin but once begun, time evaporated. After five or six hours of writing, it was time to put the computer away. Only writers know how exhausting that activity can be. The brain hums, the muscles tense. Then it was time for a hike around the park, or maybe a trek down to the little market about a half mile away. I then prepared a small supper, watched the evening news, took a shower, got into bed, read for a while and fell asleep. The simple life!

It had been two months since I set out from Greenville to "discover America" and also to "discover me." I'd watched the landscape change in more ways than one. It was a different country from when I began. In many ways, I was also becoming a different person.

The latest news was that two postal workers in Washington D.C. had died from inhalation of anthrax. I couldn't understand why the—*terrorists*—hated America so much. No one yet had a clear idea of who they were or what their anger was about. Not even the TV journalists seemed to know. It seemed that every day America braced for another attack. National anxiety was pandemic. Yet my own life had settled into a simple and peaceful rhythm. In the larger context of my country, it was a dramatic and stressful time. The juxtaposition of personal peace with national angst was odd; it was also creatively invigorating.

The week at Rancho Los Coches turned into the most productive phase of my "sabbatical." The weather was perfect and it was extremely pleasant there. It was just me, my computer and the cozy confines of the RV. I sometimes sat at the picnic table outside or took long walks along the paths that led to the nearby stream and boulders. I left windows and skylights open and enjoyed many species of birds fluttering and chirping in the surrounding trees.

Several of those days I visited with Laurie. Laurie and I had first met in a writing workshop at the University of Texas at Dallas in 1986 when both of us were "returning" students. Since then I'd watched her completely transform herself, changing from a shy high school drop-out to an accomplished professional woman and political activist. She and her ex-husband Bill had been divorced for nearly fifteen years but they still lived together. As Laurie explained it, "We get along better divorced than we ever got along while married."

Bill and Laurie took me to San Diego Harbor for Mexican beer and seafood at their favorite restaurant. We were at a table overlooking the water when a huge elephant seal breached the waves. There were lots of oohs and ahs from diners. That was one more example of marine life that I'd never before seen—or expected to see. After lunch, they took me on a quick tour of the downtown area and then to their house in the Pacific Beach neighborhood.

The house where they lived was tiny and shabby-chic. Its main attraction was a location only two blocks from the ocean. They said they paid $1200 a month rent and that was considered inexpensive. Bill said the house would easily sell for $375,000. They got a deal, he explained, because he did electrical work on other rental properties for the owner-landlord. The prices of real estate in California were skyrocketing. I'd already learned that from Robin. It was obvious that Laurie and Bill loved their Pacific Beach bungalow. The neighborhood was one of those quirky places that attract the Bohemian crowd. I marveled that Bill, the good-ole-boy-ex-redneck from Texas, felt so at home in that community. Laurie, on the other hand, was finally in her natural element.

Since our schooldays in Texas, Laurie had become a nationally recognized scholar on ethnic women's literature. It amazed me to realize that she was the same Laurie with the deep Texas twang and bad grammar I'd first met. The youngest of six children, no one in the family had finished high school--not even Laurie. She'd married Bill when she was 17 and had her first baby at 18. But there had always been something in Laurie that made her yearn for more than what she experienced in rural Texas. She'd always loved to read and through reading realized how much more the world had to offer. Without Bill's support, she got her GED and enrolled in community college in Dallas. She did so well scholastically that she transferred easily to the upper level University of Texas at Dallas and graduated there with honors. Then she went on to finish master's and doctorate degrees at North Texas University. Now she was the published author of four scholarly books.

Laurie's ex-husband Bill had been a typical Texas "good-old-boy." He worked as a telephone lineman, and had at one time been abusive to Laurie. When she got the guts to leave him, Bill was so upset that he followed wherever she moved. As Laurie became more successful and self-confident, Bill's anger and jealousy changed to pride. "Bill got an education along with me," Laurie said. "What I learned, I taught to him, and it opened up his closed mind. My education changed us both." About five years before Bill had had a stroke that left him blind in one eye. Then he had triple bypass surgery. Laurie nursed him through each of his medical crises but she drew the line at remarrying.

After being together for many years, Laurie and Bill were mutually supportive and more passionate than ever. Bill mostly stayed home and took care of household matters in order to free Laurie for her professorship at San Diego State as well as union lobbying duties in Sacramento. Instead of disparaging him for the role he'd assumed, Laurie was grateful. When invited to business dinners, etc., she insisted Bill be included. "He's bored at home all day doing drudge work and I know how important it is to get out and go to nice places and interact with other adults. I understand because I used to stay home," Laurie insisted.

Laurie handled most of their business matters, and when an investor group in Texas offered one million dollars for property they'd paid $79,000 for eleven years earlier, Laurie threw them out of the house. She refused to go forward with the deal after the men criticized Bill for letting his wife handle negotiations. "You don't treat Bill like that!" she screamed. "Go fuck your million dollars!" She meant it, too. Now she refused to talk to the investors and said she was saving the property for retirement. "If those guys were willing to pay a million dollars, well, somebody else will be willing later. Anyway what the hell would me and Bill do with that kind of money? We wouldn't know how to spend it." Bill amiably agreed.

Both Bill and Laurie were good looking people. Bill had wavy gray hair and a beard. His body was still trim and muscular. Laurie was slender, with long brown hair and skin free of make-up. While Bill was taciturn, she was full of colorful expressions. She said many of her university colleagues didn't know what to make of her. In spite of having a doctorate in English, Laurie still spoke with a thick Texas accent and used lots of colloquialisms. In fact, I suspected her of laying it on extra thick just for effect.

"When someone asks why I talk the way I do," she smiled, "I tell them it took me many long years to master this dying dialect and I have no intention of giving up a skill that required such time and effort to perfect!"

CHAPTER 11

PRAISING ARIZONA

I finally took my leave of California by heading east on Interstate 8, first going over mountains and driving through the Cleveland National Forrest. I passed the Campo and Manzanita Indian Reservations. There was a long descent into the beautiful Imperial Valley with the highway median sometimes so wide that westbound lanes weren't visible from the eastbound. The terrain was mostly treeless and hilly with lots of rock outcroppings. Sometimes the highway came within a half mile of the Mexican border.

I crossed the California state line at the Colorado River and on the other side was Yuma, Arizona. Yuma looked intriguing on the map but from the Interstate seemed to be one long corridor of trailer parks. All I could see was flatland and trailers—a metropolis of snowbirds.

That afternoon I exited the Interstate at Gila Bend, Arizona. I liked the romantic sound of the name, like an old-time rough-and-ready cowboy town. First thing I noticed was a dilapidated sign that read "Gila Bend Welcomes You, Home of 1700 people and five old crabs." It was scorching hot as I drove down the broad main street that loosely followed railroad tracks. Spindly palm trees were planted here and there along the way. There was a McDonald's and Burger King, several gas stations and used car lots and one place with a collection of metal dinosaurs out front. There were a number of boarded up businesses. The busiest place in town seemed to be *Rosalita's, Cold Beer Anytime.*

Temps were in the high 90's when I finally pulled into the dusty little RV Park. Mexican music was playing and a jolly group of friends were gathered around a barbecue grilling meat and drinking cervezas. After getting hooked up, I closed my windows, revved up the AC, got out my atlas and tried to figure out where to go next. As soon as the sun went down, the temperature plummeted and it was finally comfortable enough to open the windows. As usual, I turned in early.

Heading east the next day, the Sonora Desert became more impressive. There were lots of tall saguaro cacti and I passed the Maricopa Mountains. It was picture postcard American desert country. I continued on I-8 until it merged into I-10 near Casa Grande. Then I traveled 10 through Tucson. From my freeway vantage point, Tucson was a nice middle-sized city. The weekend traffic was light. Soon I was past Tucson and back in the desert. The weather was exceedingly hot and windy; as I drove along, the RV occasionally shook and swayed from the force of wind gusts.

About 40 miles east of Tucson I turned south onto Arizona State Highway 80 and drove 22 miles to Tombstone. I hooked up for the night at a park on the edge of the historic town center and walked only a few blocks till I was in the middle of everything. The main street of Tombstone was bustling with tourists. Besides English, I heard German, French, Italian and Spanish being spoken. It was surprising to find so many Europeans in such an out of the way place. I figured it must be the western movie influence that enticed them there.

In the late nineteenth century, Tombstone had the wildest reputation of all the western towns. After gold and silver were discovered in the area, it attracted thousands of adventurers and outlaws. Tombstone was where Johnny Ringo and Doc Holliday were the most infamous resident gunfighters. The female population was small and feuds over women were common. Saloons stayed open 24-hours a day and houses of prostitution operated openly. It was the town where in 1884 the Earp and Clanton brothers shot it out at the OK Corral. But the Tombstone I explored in 2001 was a town dedicated to tourism.

I walked for hours looking at restored historical buildings such as the Birdcage Theater and Tombstone Epitaph News. I wrote and mailed about 20 postcards because I wanted the Tombstone postmark on them. Back in the RV, I followed my usual routine of a light supper followed by watching the news on TV, then climbed into my cozy loft for reading and sleep. By eight o'clock next morning, I had already finished cleaning, stowing and disconnecting the RV, and was once again on the road. But before leaving Tombstone, I stopped at Boot Hill just outside town.

Being an aficionado of graveyards and the tales they tell, Boot Hill was an interesting storybook. I spent a long time meandering and reading grave markers. A lot of it was garishly restored—a cemetery theme park—but there was still enough of the real thing remaining to keep my interest. I liked the way many epitaphs hinted at so much more. One read "Lynched by the Benson Mob, 1880. " Another said "Murdered 1891," and another simply stated, "Killed by Indians." There were segregated sections of the cemetery for "disreputable ladies" and another for citizens of Chinese descent. I took a picture of one shabby metal cross in the area for prostitutes that read simply, "Dutch Annie, 1888." A more elaborate headstone in the Chinese section was inscribed "Mrs. Ah Lum (China Mary), Born China, died in Tombstone, Dec. 16, 1906."

After leaving Boot Hill I returned the twenty or so miles to busy Interstate 10. My plan was to drive only a short distance on 10, then take scenic U.S. 191 to northern Arizona. I hadn't studied the map carefully and was completely unaware how mountainous the terrain ahead was. All I noticed were the green dots signifying a scenic byway and that was enough to send me on my way. The road went through the Apache National Forest and was part of the Apache Nation. I figured it would be an interesting and picturesque several hour drive.

The roads I followed were almost devoid of other vehicles. Once I came to a crossroads that stretched for long vacant miles in all four directions. I pulled to the side of the road, marveling at how vast and empty the land was. I called my friend Barbara in Newnan,

Georgia, and we chatted for a while about my travels. She asked lots of questions and wanted to know where I was headed next. I replied that I wasn't precisely sure. All I knew was that I was contentedly headed due north and planned to follow the green dotted scenic route to wherever it took me. My crossroads telephone break was in country as remote and desolate as any place I'd yet encountered.

There were several historical markers along the way explaining that the territory had first been traversed and described by Spanish explorer Francisco Vasquez de Coronado in 1540. It was later scouted and mapped by Kit Carson. The highway had formerly been US 666 and nicknamed "the devil's highway." In 1992 it was changed to 191, The Coronado Trail. I later learned it was the least traveled federal highway in America.

At the beginning 191 consisted of open prairie with buttes, mesas, and purple mountains in the distance. Nothing stood out until I reached the copper mining town of Clifton. I was aghast at how ravaged the land was around Clifton. There had been continuous strip mining there since 1872 and the town was surrounded by huge open pits. The copper mine there is the largest and deepest in the United States and one of the biggest in the world.

Clifton reminded me of a place in a science fiction film. Whole mountainsides were sliced away. As I drove into town there was a sign posted at the only service station I saw: "Next Gas 100 miles." My tank was a little less than half full, so I decided to fill up. But it was Sunday and the station was closed. No big deal, off I headed up Arizona Hwy 191 with no idea what lay ahead.

Clifton was at the base of the San Francisco Mountain Range that began an abrupt climb just over the San Francisco River on the northern edge of town. I soon realized I was on perhaps the most challenging drive of my trip, more daunting than the Rocky Mountains or coastal cliffs in northern California. A distance I thought would take several hours to cover ended up taking six grueling hours of white knuckle concentration.

The scenery, however, was breathtaking. Unlike most scenic routes, there were few or no places to pull off the road and photograph the incredible vistas. At times the two narrow lanes hugged a mountainside climbing upward on one side and dropping deep into heavily forested ravines on the other. My imagination ran wild. I thought it possible to go off one of those precipices and not be found for years, maybe never. And no one knew where I was. But what could I do? There was nowhere to stop and turn around and my cell phone was out of range. All I could do was keep going, hope for the best and marvel at nature's beauty.

The road grade was continuously steep with numerous switchbacks and hairpin curves. I drove over many peaks and when I thought I was finally over the final one, another would rise ahead. On one particularly tight curve the RV's kitchen cabinet popped open and spilled out its contents. "Unbreakable" glasses and dishes crashed and splintered. From then on I had to listen to the broken pieces rattling from side to side as I maneuvered each turn.

I kept an eye on the altimeter which eventually registered near 8800 feet. Then finally the mountains leveled into a grassy plateau called Hannagan's Meadow, and just beyond there was the village of Alpine. In Alpine I was finally able to buy gas; I put 33-plus gallons into the 35-gallon tank.

It was dark when I finally reached Holbrook, Arizona. The main street was part of historic Route 66. Murphy's Law continued to plague me. At the campground north of town, it was too dark to find my assigned site. Other campers helped search but they couldn't find it either. When finally I did locate the spot and start to hook up in pitch dark, the water faucet was too far away for my hose to reach, so I had to unhook electricity and cable and find another spot. The park was far from full so there was no problem settling anywhere. I chose a location under some scraggly trees. Then I faced the irksome task of cleaning up the broken dishes. Plastic and glass shards were imbedded all over the carpet. Most of these had to be picked out by hand wearing leather work gloves.

As luck would have it, it was the night for daylight savings time to fall back an hour. But because I had crossed into the Mountain Time Zone that day, my clock stayed the same. No gaining an extra hour for me. On the entire trip I had never felt so utterly weary and relieved to be stopped and settled for the night. I was too tired for supper and reading, so climbed gratefully into my comfy loft and fell instantly asleep.

The next morning I awoke feeling refreshed and eager to figure out what next. The weather in Holbrook was mild and the campground, although far from bucolic, was cheap and pleasant. A young Hopi woman ran the office. She was friendly and helpful and sold baskets, jewelry and petrified wood as a sideline. The best thing was that there was nowhere I had to be and nothing I had to do. I decided to stay put for a few days; doing nothing for a while had great appeal.

The camper parked closest to me was occupied by a retired couple from Canada. We introduced ourselves and that night they invited me over to share their campfire. While discussing our traveling experiences, I told them about my harrowing trip up 191. They were amazed that I'd driven the road in an RV and wanted to hear all about it. They told me that they'd been advised not to attempt it with their fifth wheel trailer. Their tour book called it the most difficult but also the best driving road in America. My reaction to that was, *Wow...more serendipity.* When I'd impulsively decided to follow those little green dots I had no idea of what lay ahead. Now that it was over, I was thrilled that I'd had the experience.

I ended up staying three nights in Holbrook. Finally, though, I was ready to be on the move again. I took Interstate 40 and drove 26 miles to the Petrified Forest National Park. The entrance fee was $10 and I was one of the few visitors there. The first six miles of the park wandered through the lower edge of the Painted Desert, a picturesque high plateau of brilliantly variegated buttes and mesas that extended 150 miles north and west to the Grand Canyon. The colors in the Painted Desert were lovely and subtle, with striations of shale, marl and limestone in shades of red, blue, yellow, lavender and white. I had seen similar desert strata as I passed between Hannagan's Meadow and Holbrook but not as beautiful as this.

All along I-40 before reaching the park entrance, there were petrified logs lying in segments behind ranch fences, sometimes with cattle grazing around them. I think there may have been more petrified trees on the private land I passed than I saw in the park. That was probably because visitors have carted away hundreds of thousands of tons of souvenirs over the years since the park opened in 1906. At one time, no one gave a thought to taking as many fossils as they wanted, until the losses began noticeably depleting the forest. Eventually a law was passed to forbid the removal of souvenirs. Signs posted warned of a heavy fine or even jail time for those caught stealing.

There were still plenty of petrified trees in the park. The most interesting thing to me, however, was the petroglyphs pecked into the black rock varnish that naturally coated many of the desert boulders. The petroglyphs were carved by Native Americans over a period of hundreds, even thousands of years. One of the goals of my trip had been to seek out American art but I never thought about petroglyphs. The primitive pictures carved into rock turned out to be some of the most fascinating American art that I encountered.

Petroglyphs are a form of ancient record keeping or graffiti usually made by males marking territory, memorializing an event or creating a calendar to track the yearly movement of the sun across the sky. There was a big difference in skill level between the various "artists." Some petroglyphs were poorly executed and it was impossible to tell what they were—often just geometric squiggles and spirals. Others were quite sophisticated in portraying humans and animals. Most common were hunting and animal scenes, but there were also domestic pictures and crude maps. There are literally thousands of petroglyphs in the Petrified Forest National Park.

A brochure I picked up explained that there is no word or concept in Native languages for art or artist. Artistry is simply regarded as good skill—at rock carving, pottery, basket weaving, making fetishes, dancing, or whatever. The most admired skill in early Indian cultures was hunting. Some of the petroglyphs I saw dated to the time of Christ so that was definitely the oldest "American art" I expected to see even if the artists did not consider it such!

I drove for more than 20 miles into the park, often getting out of the RV to explore more closely. I hiked several marked paths to archeological sites of ancient dwelling places. All along the way were big black ravens perched on rocks and walls. They seemed unafraid of humans.

Then I returned to I-40 and continued east. There was open range on both sides of the highway and the wind was whipping. Tumbleweeds somersaulted across the Interstate, ignored by speeding drivers. I became intrigued with how some of the tumbleweeds missed car after car, rolling unscathed to the other side through six lanes of traffic and then continuing their way across the plain. Others got snagged by undercarriages or hitched for a while stuck to grills and bumpers.

CHAPTER 12

THE LAND OF ENCHANTMENT

That night I made it to Red Rock State Park, just over the state line in New Mexico. The setting was spectacular beneath massive Church Rock, a Zuni and Navajo holy place. There were red cliffs on three sides of the camp, with a view of three-towered Church Rock pointing into the sky like an ethereal adobe castle.

About 9 PM came a sharp rap at my door. It was Joan, who irritably informed me that I had "stolen" her camping spot. She had temporarily left that morning in her small motorhome to explore northward and had returned to find me usurping her prime location. I explained that the woman working in the camp office had told me to take any empty spot I found. Joan's "Occupied" sign had apparently disappeared in the wind.

I apologized and offered to unhook and move. Joan and I began talking—she also was on a trip by herself and had already been at Red Rock for several days. She was on her way from Oklahoma to visit her son in California. Although originally peeved at me, she changed her mind and told me not to bother moving, that she'd find another spot for the night. But I insisted upon giving back the campsite and came outside to unhook connections. We were still chatting amiably as I unhooked the water. "Be careful with that handle, it's been giving me problems," Joan cautioned, but not soon enough. The metal spigot broke off in my hand and water suddenly sprayed in a high-pressured arc into the desert. There was no shut-off valve. I tried my best to forcibly replace the handle and got thoroughly soaked, all to no avail. Joan went to get the camp manager, who said he'd have to call an emergency plumber to come all the way from Gallup.

As it turned out, Joan and I both had to move to new places and we settled in next door to each other. The plumber arrived several hours later, but not before thousands of gallons of precious water had gushed onto the bone dry ground, forming a muddy bog where the best campsite had been.

While awaiting the plumber, Joan and I sat at a picnic table and chatted. We were sitting there when two people wandered up wanting to know what all the commotion was about. They introduced themselves as Jim and Louise from Dallas. Jim told us that he worked as a stage lighting director for big rock concerts. He said he was fifty-four years old, but he looked older with his long gray hair, Fu Manchu mustache and goatee. Louise explained that she was a freelance graphic artist and frequently consulted in New York on catalog design. Jim had picked her up that afternoon at the Albuquerque Airport where she'd flown in from New York. She said that very morning she'd visited "Ground Zero" in Manhattan and was still in shock at what she'd seen.

"No matter how many images you see, nothing compares with the horror of actually staring into that giant, grisly, rubble-filled hole," she said. "And the smell is horrible. It made me gag. It smells like death."

"No wonder it smells," said Jim. "It's a grave. A massive open grave."

Jim was drunk. He was energetic, talkative and witty, but very, very drunk. He admitted that he'd already undergone hip replacement surgery due to tissue necrosis caused from alcohol abuse, and he might have to have another operation soon. Fifty-four years old or not, Jim was like a big, gangly, genial kid, with his main topics of conversation being rock music, rock musicians and getting high. He was funny but also sad. Louise shrugged at whatever outrageous thing he had to say.

The four of us sat at the picnic table under the stars and talked for a long time, until the plumbers finished repairing the water spigot. Then Jim, Louise and Joan drifted away, leaving me still wide awake. I got out my journal and wrote about the day. It was nearly 2 AM. For all the trouble that had occurred, it had been an entertaining evening and I'd met some interesting people who I knew I'd remember for a long time.

Late the next morning I said good-bye to Jim, Louise and Joan and again headed for the highway. I didn't plan to drive far, just from Red Rock to Albuquerque. Several miles down the road from Church Rock, however, I happened upon the Navajo Cultural Center and Museum. The museum was featuring an exhibit of black and white photography from the 1930's and 40's of reservation life. The photos had been made by a native amateur photographer named Snow. Of course I had to stop and have a look. They were elegant photographs. I remarked on how good I thought they were to a woman who was viewing the exhibit at the same time. "Thank you," she said, "The photographer was my father."

After leaving the museum, I continued for a while on I-40, then left to travel the rest of the way into Albuquerque on Route 66. Route 66 had occasional abandoned gas stations and other businesses along the way, only a few of which had been restored. Most were vacant, weathered and falling apart. Very little traffic passed on what was once called "America's Road." It was the highway Jack Kerouac and Neal Cassady (Sal Paradise and Dean Moriarty in the book) drove in *On The Road*. It was the highway the Okies followed in their escape from the Dust Bowl during the Depression. It was also the great pathway of opportunity that led from Chicago and the Midwest to the golden opportunities of California. I stopped to take a photograph at the picturesque Continental Divide Indian Trading Post, a derelict "tourist trap" and gas station left over from Route 66's heyday. It seemed to be completely deserted.

I was busy snapping pictures when out of nowhere two Indian men appeared and stood closely on each side of me. I felt a rush of fear, their actions were menacing and they reeked of alcohol. I thought at the very least I was about to lose my expensive 35-milimeter camera.

One mumbled, "Our car ran out of gas and we need money to buy gas. We're stranded." He uttered a few more words that I couldn't understand, never looking me in the eye. Then he blurted, "I'm sorry to beg." Of course, that's what they were doing, begging for booze money. There was no "out of gas" car in sight and no traffic in either direction on Route 66. The abandoned station probably hadn't sold gas for about forty years. I was alone with two drunk Indians and my heart was hammering. What should I do?

In a friendly voice that belied how I felt, I said, "Sure, I'll help you with gas." I quickly decided this was no time to be snooty. I didn't want to insult them by not giving them enough money and I didn't want to give them so much that they'd think I was flush. My thoughts raced--*How much for a bottle of cheap booze?*

"I'll pay you to let me take your pictures," I offered. Then suddenly they were all smiles, no longer begging but earning money by posing. "Sure, sure, take our picture." They stood in front of the trading post and I snapped a few quick shots. Then I dug in my wallet and handed them a ten dollar bill. That seemed to do the trick. They were all smiles, thanking me politely as I quickly got back into my RV and drove away. The last I saw of them was a reflection in the rearview mirror as they waved goodbye.

Later I wondered if perhaps that was a scam they regularly worked. Hang out at the old trading post that sits atop the continental divide and wait for tourists to stop for pictures. Because I was alone I felt threatened—a scary feeling—but the more I thought about it they had never actually been threatening. Chalk that experience up to one more lesson learned!

That night was Halloween but I didn't remember until the next morning. On the radio they were discussing what a dud it had turned out to be, with many parents keeping their kids home from trick-or-treating due to general post Nine Eleven angst. Being that cautious seemed an over-reaction to me. Halloween had always been one of my kid's favorite holidays.

On the outskirts of Albuquerque I stopped and bought Navajo fry bread from a woman at her roadside stand. It was like a puffy fried tortilla heaped with beans, chopped lettuce, tomato and onions. Greasy, tasty and filling. I could also have gotten the fry bread sprinkled with cinnamon and sugar. It was another new food I sampled on my trip; something I probably wouldn't have had the chance to otherwise try.

I followed I-40 into the middle of Albuquerque then exited onto 25 North. When I reached Rio Rancho I decided I'd gone far enough and began looking for the little trailer highway sign that meant an RV campground was coming up. I followed the next sign to a park situated on land once used as a stage coach stop. It seemed a nice place to stay while I planned where to go next. I liked the feel of the camp; it was secure, clean and quiet. Although in the middle of civilization there was a great view of the Sandia Mountains to the east. Next door was an antique car museum and across the highway was a shopping center. I had a heap of laundry to catch up on and, best of all, there was a modern laundry room provided for park guests.

Feeling puny and in no hurry to be on the move again, I remained at Rio Rancho for several days. I thought maybe I was coming down with a virus. Then on the fourth morning I awoke feeling like my old self. In spite of chapped lips and a minor nosebleed caused from the ultra dry air, I again felt healthy. The girl who worked in the office told me that I'd probably been feeling the effects of altitude sickness—Rio Rancho was 6000 feet above sea level. She said lots of people go through a transition period until their bodies adjust to the high, thin air.

Good thing I was in no hurry but the feeling of returned good health made me eager to be back on the road. The kind of road trip I was on inevitably consumed more time than I thought it would. I'd finally figured out it was useless to rush, so I didn't. I was pretty relaxed about time spent and distance covered. By not hurrying I saw and experienced so many more things than I otherwise would have. And being on my own left me completely in charge of when, where, why and how far to go.

Occasionally a twinge of guilt nudged my conscience—but only a little. I recognized the "guilt" as a cultural, female thing and quickly squashed it. I refused to allow self-defeating emotions because my journey felt so right in every possible way. There was, however, an underlying feeling that my life on the road was not reality. Reality was at home. But at the same time—it was "reality" in a purer sense. I put quotation marks around "reality" because the real me and my real life was happening then and there. That other "reality" of home and work, family and friends, routine and responsibility had temporarily become the more unreal part of my life. If there is such a thing as being in the "travel zone," I was in it. I was experiencing the liberation of travel.

On Sunday afternoon I drove from Rio Rancho to Santa Fe. The short drive was a gradual climb into ever higher elevation. About halfway there my cruise control quit and the engine began knocking. Of course that concerned me but there was nothing I could do in the middle of nowhere. I kept going and eventually the knocking quit. After giving it thought, I figured the engine roughness probably resulted from the 86 octane gas I'd put in the tank. There was no 87 octane in that part of the country, a fact I thought might have to do with the altitude. And miraculously, my cruise control soon began working. I never again had trouble with it.

I hooked up at a nondescript campground close to town and next morning took a shuttle to the city center. I spent all morning playing the tourist role, wandering the central plaza looking at jewelry, baskets and pottery offered for sale along the sidewalks. After lunch I walked several blocks to the Georgia O'Keefe Museum. Very few people were there. That gave me the opportunity to stand as long as I wanted in front of each painting, looking to my heart's content. No museum docents rushed visitors along. I ended up spending several contented hours there.

The next day I returned downtown and this time purchased a small black pottery bowl and inexpensive Navajo-style rug that fit perfectly in the RV. Then I treated myself to a fabulous lunch at Patito Restaurant. I spent the rest of the afternoon at the Santa Fe Museum of Fine Arts which was hosting an exhibit of paintings by Emily Carr, Georgia O'Keefe and Frida Kahlo called A Room of Their Own. It was fantastic to find three of my favorite painters grouped together in one venue.

I arrived back at the RV pleasantly tired after walking around for more than five hours. There was still plenty of daylight to write in my journal and catch up on the news on TV. There was so much to see in Santa Fe I decided to stay several more days. Art was everywhere and I'd only had time to take in the largest two museums.

Next day I ventured to Site Santa Fe, an exhibit of contemporary art. I expected more of the Southwest theme but found the collection closer to what I'd seen at MassMoCA. Another day I drove to Canyon Road, an area of small, private galleries. I parked and walked what seemed like miles, going inside whatever shop or studio I found appealing. I looked at so many paintings, photographs, sculptures, baskets and pots that everything began to blur—a case of *art overload*. The weather was nice, the gallery owners were friendly and it was good exercise.

Overnight it rained and was still misting when I unhooked the RV in preparation to leave Santa Fe. I had to change out of wet clothes before heading up the highway toward Taos. It was definitely "up" because the farther north, the higher the altitude. I thought I'd already acclimated but chapped lips and minor nosebleeds continued to remind me that I was ever moving into thinner air.

The drive from Santa Fe to Taos was short. Much of the way wound through tribal land belonging to the Navajo, Zuni, Hopi and Santa Clara Indians. The scenery was magnificent. My first stop was at St. Francis Assisi Church in Rancho de Taos, just off the main highway before reaching the actual town of Taos. It would have been easy to miss but I kept a close lookout and suddenly there it was! This was the church and bell tower so often painted by Georgia O'Keefe and photographed by Ansel Adams among others.

Construction of the church began in 1772 and was finished and dedicated the first day of 1815. It had been in use by the surrounding community ever since. It was amazing to find this architectural masterpiece, world renowned as an outstanding example of adobe design and construction, in such a tiny and impoverished village. It is impossible to overstate the beauty of the building's thick, organic, curvilinear walls. No wonder O'Keefe called it "one of the most beautiful buildings left in the United States."

The whitewashed hand-carved wooden doors were unlocked and unguarded. I peeked inside, expecting at any moment to be turned back by a security guard, but instead found a silent sanctuary filled with beautiful paintings and carvings. The room was dominated by an eight-foot painting of Jesus. For many decades pilgrims have visited St. Francis of Assisi Church to view what many believe is the miracle of the glowing Jesus.

Supposedly, when the lights go out, the life-sized painting of Jesus standing by the Sea of Galilee gradually fades away as the surrounding clouds and water begin to glow. Then the image of Christ is reputed to become iridescent and three-dimensional, some claim he turns in silhouette, and a shadowy cross appears over his right shoulder. Henri Ault, who painted the picture in 1896, denied knowledge of how this phenomenon occurs; he claimed to have first seen it in his studio. It was exhibited at the 1904 St. Louis World's Fair and many there professed to have seen the "miracle." It then hung for many years in European galleries. In 1948 the painting was purchased by a wealthy Texan, Mrs. Herbert Sidney Griffin, and donated to the church in her adopted "second hometown."

Although the glowing Jesus has been examined by scientists from the nearby Los Alamos Laboratory as well as representatives of the Catholic Church, no explanation for the luminescence has been discovered. The Church prefers to call it a "mystery rather than a miracle."

I got to Taos early enough to arrange space at a campground, then go into town to explore the central plaza. It was much like Santa Fe but smaller. The next morning I set out for Abiquiu. My expectations were slight because of the commercialism I'd found in Santa Fe and Taos and I figured Abiquiu might be the same. What a surprise to find the tiny village completely unspoiled and perhaps much the same as when Georgia O'Keefe lived and worked there.

After asking directions I easily found the house where O'Keefe lived during the winter. It was enclosed by an adobe wall with only the driveway visible from the street. A car was in the driveway, apparently someone lived there. At the top of the hill beyond the house was a small cemetery where I stopped to look around. Most of the graves had handmade monuments and markers. Rocks outlined some of the plots and small gifts had been left here and there. There were candles, stuffed animals and wine bottles. This simple, overgrown graveyard overlooked a majestic panorama of desert and mountains. Alongside was a fenced meadow where several horses grazed, paying scant attention to the two border collies circling the field.

Abiquiu consisted of a combo general store/gas station and a small commercial art gallery called The Tin Moon. The store sold groceries, hardware and ranch supplies. There was also a café inside that was doing a respectable business. About five miles beyond the settlement was Ghost Ranch, where Georgia O'Keefe lived and worked three seasons of the year (moving into town only during the harsh winters). When she died, O'Keefe left Ghost Ranch to the Presbyterian Church and it has since served as a retreat and conference center. There was a small museum of Southwestern native artifacts on the property. There was also a scrubby camping area amid a clump of stunted trees.

Ghost Ranch is 40,000 acres of desert, hills, mountains and meadows. The actual location of O'Keefe's house is out of bounds to visitors. Along the road beyond the entrance gate was an abandoned settler's cabin built of hand-hewn logs. I stopped, explored and took pictures. There was no marker telling when the cabin was built or who had lived there, but it looked plenty old. Often renowned places such as Abiquiu and Ghost Ranch turn out to be less than expected but that wasn't true this time. I expected to see commercial exploitation but found the same empty and peaceful simplicity that had attracted O'Keefe there in the 1920's.

After leaving Ghost Ranch, I traveled through the Santa Clara Pueblo and stopped at several pottery studios. The "studios" were in private homes with hand-lettered signs in the front yard. These humble studios seemed incongruous with what is generally considered some of the world's most accomplished and renowned producers of art pottery. The Santa Clara style pots quickly became my favorite, even if out of my price range.

I wandered off the main road and happened upon the studio of Toni Roller. When I stepped inside the open gallery, Toni herself welcomed me warmly. She was generous with information, describing how she gathered clay from a secret spot high in the mountains, a place discovered by her grandmother. She explained that the dirt she used is red and lumpy when first mined. Then she begins the slow process of pulverizing and purifying. She told me that she always created her pottery by the coil (or roll—thus her name, Roller) method taught traditionally by the elder women of the tribe.

The coil method means that the potter first rolls the clay into thin ribbons and then pinches the ribbons together to create form. It's the ancient tradition of Native Americans. Traditionalists never use a potter's wheel; size and shape are constructed freehand. The artists carve ancient symbols and designs on the damp clay, then fire the pots in adobe kilns. When a piece is fired, chances are great that the pottery will break in the process. The potters sometime use the broken shards to incorporate into the adobe used to re-furbish the exterior of their church each year.

The final color of red or black is achieved in firing. The beautiful and highly prized black glaze of the Santa Claras is created from carbonization using dried, pulverized cattle manure. Toni explained that she always destroyed any pot with even the tiniest hairline fracture. If the pot survived the kiln it was then meticulously hand polished using special stones passed down for generations. Toni showed me a box of exquisite smooth stones originally used by her great grandmother. Pottery is usually made by the women of the tribe, she explained, and the pots are said to be a union of the natural element (earth, clay), artistic beauty (design, shape, color) and utilitarianism (all vessels are not only beautiful to look at but also meant for household or ceremonial use).

Toni was humble but at the same time deeply serious in explaining her work. Only later did I learn that Toni Roller pots are prized worldwide by collectors of Native American pottery. Her pottery is part of many museum collections, including the Vatican, and has also been displayed at the White House. She mentioned that she had shipped pieces to almost every continent. I would have loved to buy something but there was nothing in her modest studio priced less than $700, and most were over a thousand.

The Santa Clara Pueblo was as impoverished as other reservations but I noticed a difference. Adobe kilns were in many yards. The members of this tribe made their living by ranching and by creating beautiful pottery. There was not a gambling casino anywhere.

That afternoon I got a sad telephone message from Becky. She said that Bill's lung cancer had killed him. Such a short time ago he'd been in seemingly good health and was working a physically demanding factory job. Bill and Becky had invited me to visit their home on the river when I got to Georgia, and I had planned to do so. Now Bill was gone before I could make it that far. He was only fifty-two years old. Bill's death set off some serious reflection on my part. I had never thought of my trip as a "vacation" except in the sense of being away from everyday routine. But as time passed I understood better just how life-altering the journey had become. It seemed as if events along the way pointed repeatedly to the importance of living every day to the fullest. There's an old saying: "Short time hot, long time cold." I was finally figuring out how true that was.

The next morning the national news was full of a plane crash in New York City. A passenger jet had crashed into a Queens neighborhood and killed everyone on board as well as people on the ground. There was much speculation that terrorists had struck again. But the evening news reported the crash was an accident due to mechanical failure. That was bad enough—but brought home how nervous people had become as to when, where and how the next terrorist attack might occur.

That same day I tried to put bad news and worries out of my mind by visiting the D. H. Lawrence Ranch in the hills above Taos. Originally owned by the art patron Mabel Dodge Luhan, the ranch had been her gift to David and Frieda Lawrence as a place where the tubercular writer could live a healthy lifestyle and devote himself to his art. When Frieda died in 1956 she bequeathed the property to the University of New Mexico. To my eye it looked much the same as it must have when the Lawrence's lived there in the 1920's. It was the place that Georgia O'Keefe visited on her first trip to New Mexico in 1929.

On one side of the house was a mural of a buffalo painted by Trinidad Archulata of the Taos Pueblo, a hired hand on the ranch. The painting had been left open to the elements for almost seventy years and was beautifully weathered. I snapped several pictures and wondered how many more years before the image faded away.

Behind the main ranch house was a one-room cottage where the English-American painter Dorothy Brett had lived. I tried the front door and to my surprise, it opened. I entered and sat in the same wooden chair that Brett must have occupied thousands of times. There was a narrow single bed with indented mattress and threadbare blanket still in place. Other than the bed and chair, there was only an iron wood-burning stove; no adornment whatsoever. The tiny cabin must have been quite a contrast from the prior living arrangements of the aristocratic Lady Brett. No matter, she loved it enough to spend the rest of her life there, becoming a US citizen in 1938.

A short walk up the hill behind the house and cottage was the D. H. Lawrence Memorial, an offbeat shrine nestled in the pinon woods. Visitors had left notes, juniper berries and dollar bills on the altar and I did the same. What I particularly liked about the Lawrence Ranch was how open and *authentic* it was, not the least embellished or protected from visitors. Only a few other people were there, all of us respectful of the property.

The big pine tree that O'Keefe painted still towered by the front door and seemed to be as healthy as when the artist reclined on the bench beneath its branches and created her masterpiece "The Lawrence Tree." As D. H. Lawrence described it:

The big pine tree in front of the house, standing tall and unconcerned and alive...the overshadowing tree whose green top one never looks at.... One goes out the door and the tree trunk is there, like a guardian angel. The tree trunk, the long work table and the fence!"

Nothing had changed.

That night I had a great night's rest and next morning continued my exploration of Northern New Mexico by visiting the Taos Pueblo. Just as I arrived a student named Aspen Willow who had grown up in the pueblo was forming a tour group. It was her entrepreneurial way of making extra money for college. "No charge—you can tip me if you think I do a good job," she suggested with a big smile. I gladly joined ten or twelve others.

We first headed to the multi-storied pueblos that have existed for more than a thousand years, Aspen Willow explaining their antiquity as we walked along. "These structures hold the same official historic recognition as the Egyptian Pyramids and other ancient structures," she pointed out. "Many dwellings have been continually inhabited since the fourteenth century. They consist of two or three rooms and are passed down from one generation to the next. Every year the family re-plasters the outside adobe surface in order to maintain the three-foot deep walls which insulate interiors from both the extreme cold and extreme heat of the New Mexican climate." One family, friends of Aspen Willow, welcomed us inside their living room to see what the interior was like and invited us to take pictures. There was a roaring fire in the built-in adobe fireplace.

Next Aspen Willow led us to the newest building in the community, the Catholic Church completed in 1850 and still the center of the community. She explained how the Taos religion had evolved into a mixture of Native American spiritualism and traditional Catholicism. Church members, she said, worship Mary more than Jesus because they perceive Mary as the same Goddess Mother of Indian spirit folklore. She is seen as provider of Earth's bounty, as well as creator of continuing generations through physical birth.

Our group then explored the cemetery that surrounded the remnants of a bell tower that was part of an earlier church built in 1617. Spanish soldiers had destroyed that church and massacred more than 100 women and children who had fled there for safe haven. The slaughter was in retaliation for the murder by Taos warriors of territorial Governor Charles Bent. The cemetery and Bell Tower are considered sacred ground to the Taos people and tourists are not allowed to walk among the graves.

Finally Aspen Willow led us to a string of studios and shops where pueblo residents were crafting Native American artifacts for sale to visitors. The prices were reasonable and I purchased a drum and a tomahawk. "You are now welcome to continue exploring Taos Pueblo on your own," Aspen Willow finished her tour. "Your generosity is how many here make our living." Everyone in our group was pleased with the interesting tour and I'm sure her tips were generous.

After leaving the pueblo, I drove down the road and stopped at a café. Two young women were wandering about the grounds taking photographs. When I offered to take their picture together with their cameras, they introduced themselves as Morgan and Heather. As soon as they opened their mouths, out came pure Deep South, which of course I recognized. They told me they were seniors at Troy Sate University in Alabama. They had planned to go to Europe for a student convention but September 11 had caused the gathering to be cancelled. So instead of flying to Europe, they were traveling America's back-roads, writing and taking pictures for their graduation photojournalism project. I asked, "What do your parents think of you traveling alone so far from home?" Heather shrugged her shoulders. "Oh, our parents aren't worried. They know we're responsible and can take care of ourselves. We call home every few days."

Heather and Morgan came across as intelligent, adventurous young women with enthusiastic attitudes and very good manners. I liked them immediately. Morgan even mentioned how nice it was to meet "kindred spirits" along the way. "There are lots of us out here wandering around," she said. "We meet the nicest people everywhere we go. It's a great country!"

And I agreed.

CHAPTER 13

ADIOS TO PARADISE

Reluctantly I took my leave of New Mexico and headed south then east toward Texas. Texas felt a lot like home since I'd spent almost 18 years of my life living in Dallas and Houston. Both of my kids considered themselves Texans and all of us were graduates of the University of Texas—Matt and Leslie from Austin and I from the Dallas branch. My daughter still lived in the Houston area. I planned to make time by following I-10 across south Texas until I got to Leslie's house in Bellaire.

I'd lingered longer than planned In New Mexico. I'd followed the same general route that Coronado explored. I'd been inside thousand-year-old pueblos and gazed at the same hills and pine tree painted by Georgia O'Keefe. But it was time to move on. I spread out my maps and looked for the quickest route across Texas—not that a "quick route" existed. It would be more than a one day journey even on the Interstate. The state is so large that El Paso on the western edge is closer to San Diego, California, than it is to Beaumont on the eastern side. And Beaumont is closer to Jacksonville, Florida, than it is to El Paso.

That afternoon I made it to Anthony, still in New Mexico but almost to Texas. I spent the night within spitting distance of the state line. My luck with weather had so far been good. The only rain worth mentioning had happened on the Blue Ridge Parkway. When Jim and I were in the mountains of the Northwest, it was unseasonably warm at a time that usually brings the first snow. We had one very cold day in Omaha and that was it. The climate in Washington, Oregon, and California could not have been more pleasant. Then for the two weeks I was in northern New Mexico, the weather remained mild and balmy. Now I saw on the weather channel that it was snowing in the places I'd just left.

The RV Park where I stopped was in a location where New Mexico, Old Mexico and Texas came together. The wind was howling, rain was threatening and the temperature was plunging. All night I heard the propane furnace cycling on and about midnight sleet began to ping against the skylight just above my head.

The previous day when I'd stopped for gas, I noticed that the fuel hose was leaking again. Gasoline wasn't gushing out as it had in Los Angeles, but there was a definite trickle from underneath the chassis as I pumped gas into the tank. Something was wrong with the hose that had been replaced in Oxnard. And there I was in the proverbial middle of nowhere. I decided to try and live with the leak until I reached Houston.

I didn't like the park where I was but I also didn't want to set off with an iffy fuel hose in heavy wind and rain. So I decided to stay another day, do my laundry (almost everything was dirty) and wait out the bad weather. I was parked next to an overflowing dumpster that swarmed with black flies and I had to keep the shades closed to avoid the nasty view. Some of the flies managed to wriggle inside the RV and I was constantly chasing one of the pests with the fly swatter. When I dashed to the laundry room, I found it also filled with flies, thousands of them, buzzing all around and clinging to the walls and ceiling.

I wasn't comfortable with the characters staying in the park, either. At first I had the laundry room to myself (except for the flies, which I kept zapping with a can of Raid, when in walked a short, stocky desperado (okay, I don't know that he was a desperado but that's how he looked). He was a rough character, his complexion swarthy and crisscrossed with scars. Homemade tattoos covered both brawny arms. I was glad I was armed with the insect spray! But all the guy did was to throw some jeans and shirts in a washer with no detergent, feed the machine two quarters, and quickly leave. He acted more scared of the gringo with the bug spray than I acted toward him. I was afraid to leave my clothes in the laundry room; almost all I had with me was in those washers and dryers. After what seemed like hours, everything was finally clean and dry, and I dashed back through the rain to the snug safety of the RV.

My clean laundry finally folded and put away, the bed linen changed, fresh towels in the bath, I lay back on the sofa, wrapped myself in a fleece throw and turned on the television. I channel surfed until finding an old movie. It was *Destry Rides Again* with James Stewart and Marlene Dietrich. Fabulous movie! Nothing like a great old 30's flick to wile away a wet and cold afternoon on the Mexican border. I microwaved some popcorn, drenched it with butter, popped open a Coors Light and enjoyed myself immensely.

Next morning it was still raining but I decided to leave anyway. I departed under dismal skies and drove through El Paso in gray drizzle. Not long afterward I was crawling along I-10 in a thunderstorm. The passage through El Paso took more than an hour due to heavy traffic and road construction that had lanes blocked off. From the freeway, El Paso reminded me of Mexico, with bumper-to-bumper traffic and shantytowns clinging to hillsides. For a while I could see the muddy, shallow Rio Grande from the interstate, and on the other side of the river, Juarez, Mexico.

Ten miles further west the rain came down even harder. I slowed as 18-wheelers plowed past spewing water against my windshield. I had hoped to make it to Junction but decided the sensible thing would be to stop before I had both dark and downpour to contend with. Also, I'd lost another hour, having crossed from Mountain Time into Central. I checked into an RV park just off I-10 east of Ozona and proceeded to get drenched while connecting the water, electricity and cable.

After a warm shower, I felt better. Houston was only 400 miles away. I had tomato soup and crackers for supper, then gave in to fatigue. I climbed into my sleeping loft, read several chapters of *The Blind Assassin* and turned out the light. Overhead I watched raindrops form rivulets that squiggled off the skylight. At least the wind had died down! The gentle patter on the rooftop made a nice accompaniment to slumber and I was soon out like a log.

CHAPTER 14

WALTZING 'CROSS TEXAS

Next morning I got an early start and drove many miles through the flat, featureless terrain of West Texas. Once I reached Kerrville and New Braunfels, the scenery improved considerably. I left the interstate at Kerrville and drove downtown. When I spied a Luby's Cafeteria, I stopped for a takeout meal of fried chicken, mashed potatoes, turnip greens, black-eyed peas, stuffed jalapeno pepper, Mexican corn bread, blackberry cobbler and iced tea. I sat inside the RV and spread the feast before me on my little banquet table. Thus fortified, I was ready again to hit the road.

Houston's urban sprawl began at least thirty miles west of the city. From the wide-open spaces of west and central Texas, suddenly Houston began to happen...and happen...and happen some more. I was in nonstop civilization with its ubiquitous concrete, commerce, cars and population.

I arrived late afternoon, not the best time to be on Houston roads. My plan was to hook up at Trader's Village RV Park on the northwest side of town, and call Leslie the next morning. I wanted time to relax a bit and clean the RV after the tension of driving through rain, muck and many miles of desert. It never occurred to me that Trader's might not have a space available. When I finally got there, a line of campers had formed outside the office, and when I requested a campsite they told me there was already a wait list of eleven! I quickly discovered that "Traders Village" was a huge flea market adjacent to the RV Park, and people travelled there from all over the country to buy, sell and trade. It looked like fun—I would have enjoyed walking up and down the rows of junk and treasure— but I wasn't about to be number twelve waiting for a spot that probably wouldn't happen. It was a huge park, too, with 284 concrete spaces with full hookups.

The only thing left was to call Todd and Leslie and head immediately for their house in Bellaire. Off I took in the middle of the worst of Friday afternoon traffic, trying to merge from one slow-moving, clogged lane to another. On the way, I got a good look at the beautiful Houston skyline and passed right by the Galleria. By the time I reached Todd and Leslie's house on Elm Street, it was dark. That night I parked the RV in their driveway but slept inside in a real bed.

First order of business next morning was to do something about the still leaking fuel hose. I first wasted several frustrating hours making telephone calls, getting the runaround, collecting misinformation, and then driving unnecessary miles on unfamiliar streets in an attempt to get the hose repaired. The Chevrolet hotline told me to take the motorhome to a downtown dealership; but when I got there they informed me that they were booked solid for weeks, and anyway they didn't work on motorhomes. They told me I needed to go 20 miles north to another dealer who did work on Chevrolet trucks and vans.

I must have looked utterly dispirited because the service manager took pity and offered to have his lead mechanic slide under the chassis "just to have a look." The mechanic was a wiry little guy with a deeply lined face and gray flat-top. He looked about seventy years old but he nimbly scooted on his back under the cab. After straining and groaning for about 15 minutes and obviously doing something that required all the physical strength he could muster, he slid back out to inform me that the hose was now temporarily clamped in place. He emphasized "temporarily" and warned that it still needed to be properly repaired. "It wasn't put on right when they replaced it in California," he explained. He'd had to first disconnect and then reposition the hose where it fed into the gas tank. When I got out my checkbook to pay, the manager waved me off. I felt immensely grateful and relieved. If the mechanic hadn't jerry-rigged the apparatus, I'd have been stuck in Houston until an authorized dealer could schedule repairs which would probably be several weeks at the soonest. The mechanic also informed me that the exhaust pipe should be fixed or replaced and the tires needed rotating. "You got a sweet little rig here and she'll stay that way if you take good care of her," he advised. Then he ambled off to the back of the shop.

The service manager told me to take very seriously everything the mechanic said. "He's probably the best man who will ever look at your truck. He retired from NASCAR but didn't like not working so came to work for us. I'm lucky to have him. He's the best mechanic I ever had." I thanked him with all my heart and silently thanked whatever guardian angel had led me to that dealership and that mechanic.

The rest of the day was spent trying to get the RV back in shape for the rest of the trip. I hadn't realized so much maintenance would be needed. Time was passing rapidly and I still had things not right- -a temporarily re-clamped fuel hose, a bent exhaust pipe, and tires that were 7,000 miles overdue for rotation.

The next day was Thanksgiving and Jim flew to Houston for the holiday. Leslie and I baked three pies and made side dishes while Todd fried a turkey in the back yard under still drippy skies. Then we sat in the dining room and consumed way too much food for just four people.

As it was I ended up spending more than week in Houston. Saturday night before leaving, Leslie's friend Mike came over from Louisiana. Of her many friends, Mike was one of my favorites. What I especially liked about him was his kindness and sense of fun. Mike and Leslie had been friends since they lived in the same apartment complex before Leslie and Todd married.

Mike was only a year younger than me. He was a career naval officer, having served two tours in Vietnam and one in Desert Storm. He was the divorced father of two grown daughters, a conservative Republican—and he was gay. For most of his life Mike had lived deeply closeted but finally had come out to a select group of friends. The Navy was still unaware of his sexual orientation. Out of professional necessity it was still necessary to keep his private life discreet where his naval career was concerned. Two thousand and one was the height of Don't Ask Don't Tell.

We began the evening with Leslie, Todd, Mike, Jim and I having dinner at a Chinese restaurant. Jim and Todd then returned home to watch the ball games while Mike, Leslie and I continued the evening by hitting The Briar Patch, a gay sing-along piano bar in Montrose. We had a great time sipping martinis and singing old show tunes. What happened then was totally crazy. I was sitting next to a middle-aged guy and we were laughing and yakking when suddenly he said, "You're going to think I'm completely out of my mind but I'm serious. Will you marry me?" I said, "You're right, I think you're out of your mind." His boyfriend was standing right behind him with his arm draped around his shoulders. Need I mention my proposed "fiancée" had already consumed three or four alcoholic beverages? I laughed and told him, "Thanks, but I'm already married among other things."

He wouldn't give up, though, and this is the story he told. His mother, a wealthy widow, lived in a retirement home in Dallas. It would please her immensely if her only son would finally marry before she died. "I wouldn't bother you," he promised me. "You could do whatever you pleased...live your own life...and it would mean some money to you. After my mother passes away, we could get a divorce." We laughed about it but in a way I think he was serious. He even insisted that I take his email address and let him know if I changed my mind.

Mike, meanwhile, had struck up conversation with a young man named Greg who said he was an actor, and Greg invited us all to an after-hours cast party. Mike wrote down the address. We left the Briar Patch after midnight. I was surprised when Mike began driving down streets in Montrose, looking for the address Greg had given him. Finally we found the street and slowly drove along, looking for the house number. Way down the block was a house so lit up with Christmas lights that it looked like something from the Vegas Strip. "Surely that's not where we're going," we all said in unison.... Then, *"Oh, my god, it is where we're going!"*

Outside, the lights and decorations made "gaudy" seem understated. Inside, the house was tastefully furnished and decorated. We were welcomed with genuine friendliness by an interesting group of "theater" types, both men and women, many apparently gay. A Steinway grand piano dominated the living room and beside it was a microphone and speakers. Everyone was enjoying cocktails and singing Christmas songs. Among the party guests were lots of talented performers who took turns standing before the microphone or sitting at the piano and hamming it up. It was a surreal experience. At times I felt as if I were floating among a stage production, observing as well as taking part.

Some of the guests began singing and dancing stage numbers from *Cabaret*...several of the more obscure songs...and they knew all the words and choreography. Were these people part of the currently touring *Cabaret*? No one said and we didn't ask. I was sipping my drink and trying to act as if I went to such parties all the time. They were a talented and fun group of people and I loved being there and watching them perform. After the impromptu *Cabaret* production, some of the men began singing camped-up versions of Christmas songs. Everyone laughed raucously at the bawdy lyrics.

We returned home in the wee hours and Mike spent the night on Leslie's couch. Over coffee the next morning, he informed us that his planned retirement from the Navy, scheduled for only a month away, had been cancelled due to the war. Instead of retiring, Mike would soon be going to Lake Tahoe for special cold weather and altitude training. That meant he was probably headed to Afghanistan. Our first reaction was to express disappointment but Mike quickly hushed our concerns. Although he'd served already in two wars and had been happily looking forward to retirement, Mike said he was ready to serve again. "I want to go!" he insisted. I wondered what the people who think that gays have no place in the military would think of Mike and his contribution to America.

I'd gotten as much RV maintenance accomplished as I could— getting the tires rotated and the oil changed at least—and I was eager to again be on the road. The morning of departure I got up before dawn, my bags already packed and stowed, and I waited for

Leslie and Todd's alarm clock to sound. Rain was predicted and I wanted to get out of the city before the thunderstorms hit. By 6:50 AM I was on the 610 Loop.

Almost as soon as I pulled out of the driveway, droplets began splattering the windshield. Traffic crawled on the freeways but I made steady progress east and north. At times it poured harder than anything I'd yet encountered. I could hardly see out the windshield. I leaned forward and gripped the steering wheel—determined to make it far enough out of the city to pull over and wait out the weather. Midtown traffic was awful but once I got past that it was no better. I only felt comfortable going at a slow pace. Meanwhile gigantic trucks roared past throwing up gushers of sight-obscuring spray.

As I traveled along the Houston Ship Channel and Bay Freeway, I passed a sprawling landscape of chemical plants and oil refineries with smokestacks and storage tanks silhouetting the stormy sky. About this time, it was announced on radio that the refineries and underground pipelines around Houston were on Code Alert Orange due to a video command from Bin Laden to his followers that they should destroy America's natural gas lines in the event of his capture or death. More natural gas pipelines converge under Houston than any other place on Earth, the announcer said. Meanwhile, US aircraft continued to saturate bomb the mountains of northern Afghanistan where Bin Laden was supposedly hiding. President Bush had vowed to get him dead or alive, and since Houston was Bush's hometown, Bin Laden had specifically threatened Houston.

What irony that the very day I departed San Francisco, the bridges were threatened, and now as I drove along the Texas coast lined with refineries, they also were targeted with threats. Coincidences had occurred time and again on my journey, beginning with my unplanned trip across the George Washington Bridge and glimpse of the Twin Towers. Then came the aborted border crossing at Niagara Falls at the first rush of border security; the Golden Gate and Bay Bridge crossings; and now my travel by Houston's refineries on the very day that they were specifically threatened.

I finally reached a rest area and pulled in to wait out the stormy weather. The parking spaces were packed with other campers, cars and trucks doing the same thing. I made myself a cup of hot tea, then lay back on the sofa and snuggled in my fleece throw as the wind, rain and thunder howled and crashed outside. Almost immediately I drifted off to sleep and three hours later when I finally awoke, the rain had tapered off and most of the rest area had emptied. The only vehicles left were me and a few others. I'd slept hard, undisturbed by the coming and going of grinding gears and big diesels.   .

CHAPTER 15

YOU CAN GO HOME AGAIN

I got back onto I-10 and continued east, following the rain. I drove through Port Arthur, Beaumont, Lake Charles and Lafayette, passing more oil and chemical refineries, all seemingly in full operation. Then I crossed the 18-mile-long Atchafalaya Basin Bridge. The bridge, built on elevated pillars, provided good views of the largest swamp in America. I spied migratory birds and at least one weathered shack on stilts back among the murky water and bald cypresses.

This was a stretch of highway I'd driven many times; I was no longer in unfamiliar territory. I made it only as far as Port Allen where I stopped at the first RV Park I came to. I had a tuna fish dinner, watched television and made phone calls. Then I crawled into my comfy loft and read for a while, relaxed but not sleepy. As much as I'd loved my long visit with Leslie and Todd, it felt good to be on my own again and back "on the road."

At Baton Rouge I crossed the Mississippi River before turning south toward New Orleans. At Mandeville I got onto the southbound side of the Lake Ponchatrain Causeway and after 23 miles over water exited at Metairie. I had just crossed the longest bridge in the world. I then stayed on 1-10 through the heart of New Orleans, driving as slowly as I dared, trying to see as much as I could. I wanted to get off the freeway but figured my Four Winds would be too cumbersome for the narrow streets of the old city. From the

Interstate I was able to get passing glimpses of Magazine and Canal Streets, the Fauberg Treme and Vieux Carre—all places I'd known well when I lived in New Orleans as a young woman. I then re-crossed Lake Pontchartrain on the parallel northbound bridge.

Intermittent showers continued but nothing to compare to what I'd experienced outside Houston. It had finally quit raining and the wind was whipping when on a long flat stretch of I-10 in Mississippi I noticed flashing lights in my rearview mirror. My heart did a flip-flop. I knew I was going only about 65 in a 70 zone. When the trooper approached my window, I handed him my driver's license and registration and asked why he'd stopped me. "You were wobbling," he answered. Then he asked all sorts of odd questions: where was I coming from, what was my destination and why was I traveling alone? I didn't like the questions. What business was it of his where I was going or that I was traveling alone?

As we were talking a big gust of wind came up and the RV, although stopped, gave a lurch. "Hmmm, I see what you mean," the trooper said, and from that point on he was very polite. My Four Winds was far from aerodynamic and therefore affected in a big way by wind gusts. So the state trooper probably did see me "wobble" but that's not why he stopped me. I think he stopped me because I was going less than the speed limit and he suspected I might be a drug runner. I later heard that law officers stop a lot of vehicles coming out of Texas on I-10; it's a notorious drug corridor between Mexico and the Southern and Eastern U.S.

I quickly crossed the state of Mississippi, enjoying the magnolias planted along the highway. Through Gulfport, Biloxi, Gautier and Pascagoula, the highway skirted the Gulf of Mexico, and there were more bridges to cross. I arrived in Mobile just in time for five o'clock traffic. Finally, I found my way to my friends Tim and Sue's house, parked in front, and had a wonderful dinner with them. Tim then had to leave for rehearsal for a community play he was in (*The Man Who Came to Dinner*). Sue mixed a batch of Belvedere martinis, which we proceeded to consume, and then she made another shaker full. We sipped our martinis and talked and talked. With her background in psychology, Sue always had a knack for drawing out and offering information that was interesting.

The next morning Sue and I continued our talkathon over breakfast. Then she took me to her salon for a badly needed haircut. Carol, the hairdresser, gave a good haircut and asked lots of questions about my trip. She called a bunch of people over and told them what I was doing and they made a big fuss. "You need to write a book," Carol said. "But I haven't really done anything to write about," I answered. "I've done such unexciting things." "We think it's interesting," they insisted. "We want to read the book!"

About 11 AM I returned to the RV, said goodbye to Sue (Tim was at work), and headed east again on I-10. I'd decided my next destination was Jacksonville. But after thinking a bit—I abruptly reversed course and drove north. Although I very much wanted to touch all four corners of the country by going to Jacksonville, I decided it would be better to head north. I wanted to go to Birmingham and Jacksonville was too far out of the way. I had to make a decision one or the other because time was growing short. It was December already.

I found my way back along Battleship Causeway and through the tunnel under the Mobile River to connect with I-65 toward Montgomery. After crossing the beautiful General Wilson Bridge over the Tensaw River delta, came sparse traffic, few settlements and many thick pine forests. I saw lots of flatbed trucks loaded with skinned logs on their way to lumber mills, and other big open trucks loaded with pine chips on their way to ships in the Port of Mobile and thence to China, Japan and other far destinations.

As I passed through Montgomery I thought of the interesting people who have come from or made their marks there: people like Martin Luther King, Zelda Fitzgerald and Hank Williams. About an hour past Montgomery, I pulled off the road at an RV facility and discovered I was near Auburn University. The park was in a pretty, wooded location and I noticed that some of the trailers seemed to be rented to students. I'd stopped early because I saw that the park had cable television and I didn't want to miss Survivor on television that night. Anyway, I was quite tired after all the martinis and therapeutic conversation of the previous night! Also it had begun to rain again--not my favorite driving condition.

Once I got cable hooked up and turned on the television to check the weather report, I learned that violent storms, including tornadoes, were predicted for central Alabama. Yikes!—made me double glad that I'd stopped. Within minutes the park manager rapped at the door, she was informing campers that a tornado watch was in effect. She said there was a warning siren on the property and if it sounded everyone should immediately seek shelter in the shower room. "It's really not that good in there but it's still lots safer than a trailer," she cautioned. What a welcome! Still, I felt there was no use worrying about something as unpredictable and uncontrollable as a tornado. It was fortunate I'd stopped at a facility equipped with a warning siren.

That afternoon and night the worst storms missed us to the north and I was able to sleep for eight restful hours. It was warm, quiet and peaceful inside the RV. There was nothing to wake me: no alarm clock, no lawn mowers, no telephone, no crowing roosters, not a hungry cat begging to be fed. Just the soft rustling of nearby trees and the melodious morning chirps of birds.

I had planned to visit Becky at Bill's place south of Columbus, Georgia that day but when I reached Becky on her cell phone, she said that she'd left the lake and was back in Greenville. So I headed straight up Hwy 280 toward Birmingham. Two-eighty was the old Florida Short Route, the same highway that my family took when we set out for Pensacola each summer when I was a child. Back then I thought it was the most fabulous and exciting road in the world. I remember sitting in the backseat of the car, windows open to warm blowing air, spellbound by the passing scenery on that magic gateway to the Sunshine State.

Two eighty had once been the most dangerous highway in Alabama. In the 20's through the 60's it was a two-lane blacktop that began on Birmingham's Southside and wound first through the mountains, alongside the waterworks, and then twisted its way to the Georgia line near Phenix City. At that point it was necessary to pick up other rural highways that gradually led south. No wide Interstates then!

I remembered the country gas stations where we stopped. They all seemed to have a weathered red Coca-Cola sign painted on the side and a refrigerated cooler by the front door. What a treat to reach in and pull out an icy bottled drink that frosted as soon as it hit the summer air. There were also several roadhouses along the way—we called them "honky-tonks"—colored lights strung along their rooflines and gravel parking lots with pickup trucks. We frequently passed shotgun houses with people sitting on the porches watching the cars go by. They waved and we waved back. Sometimes we'd pass prisoner chain gangs cutting brush along the highway with hand scythes. Daddy and Uncle Gordon would give us packs of Camel cigarettes to toss out the window to the convicts. Most of all, I remembered the deep piney woods along 280 and the meandering, muddy creeks.

As I drove along 280 I searched in vain for all those well-remembered sights. The creeks and woods were still there but everything else looked new and shiny. I thought, *Aren't memories usually the other way around, with things in reality being smaller and shabbier than remembered?* I searched in vain for abandoned motor courts, gas stations or jook-joints. They'd all been demolished. And instead of prisoners cutting brush with hand tools, big tractors driven by uniformed county maintenance employees mowed the grass along the roadside.

I finally stopped at a Super Wal-Mart on a stretch of 280 near Sylacauga called the "Jim Nabors Highway." The parking lot was packed with the cars of holiday shoppers. It reminded me how close it was getting to Christmas. I walked across the highway and ate lunch at Popeye's Fried Chicken. It was as greasy and good as I remembered. But all the filling stations, motor courts and honkytonks along the Florida Short Route had been replaced with big box stores and giant multi-pump convenience store stations. Instead of weathered shacks and cotton farms there were neat tract subdivisions and doublewide trailers.

I hooked up that night in Pelham. When I was growing up Pelham was a sleepy country village with one redbrick schoolhouse and not much else; now it was just another upscale suburb south of Birmingham. It had become a sprawling bedroom community of neighborhoods with names like Royal Oaks and Chandalar.

I called the secretary at work and she informed me that business had all but dried up since 9-11. She said there hadn't been enough work to keep everyone busy. "Well I hope I still have a job!" I joked. "I really can't answer that," she answered, a little too seriously. "You'll just have to take that up with Dan and he's out of the office."

Uh, oh! I thought. *This doesn't sound so good....*

The next morning I called Enterprise Rent-a-Car and had them deliver a Ford Escort two-door. Then I set out to visit my favorite aunt. She had always been the backbone of our family, a successful career woman with a strong and dynamic personality. I had spent many happy days visiting her, Uncle Gordon and my cousins in their Bluff Park home.

Aunt Frances had recently moved into "assisted living." Her new "home" was nice but it was still a shock to see her there. When someone you remember as bright, energetic and always busy—to suddenly see that person physically frail and disoriented was unnerving. The facility where she lived was nicely decorated but still seemed more hospital than home. She called her simply furnished room her "apartment" but there was little of Frances in that sterile space. She had always been someone who loved and took a great deal of pride in her surroundings. She'd made arrangements herself to go into the facility before age became a burden. Her son was living far away and she didn't want to leave the city where she'd spent most of her life. We kept the conversation as light and positive as possible but her despondency was obvious. Her eyes had lost their sparkle.

When I entered the lobby, Frances was waiting with the same bright and welcoming smile that had been a big part of my childhood. She looked fragile and thin. Holding my hand, she showed me around the dining area and library, pointing with pride to the professionally decorated Christmas tree. But she could hardly wait to be gone from the place and eagerly informed me that her friend Margie was expecting us for dinner. So after a short visit in her "apartment," we headed in my rental car up Shades Mountain to Bluff Park.

On the way, we stopped at a CVS Pharmacy to buy film so I could take pictures. We walked up and down the isles looking at things—Frances had always loved shopping and even being in a CVS seemed to be a treat to her. I bought her a box of Whitman's Sampler candy and tears came to her eyes. She acted as if I'd given her the best gift in the world. She could hardly wait to share it with Margie.

As we were slowly making our way back to the car, someone called out, "Is that Frances?" I turned and answered, "Yes, it is." "I'm Blanche," the voice responded. "Maybe she doesn't remember me." "Well, I remember you!" I said.

I escorted Frances to the car and Blanche parked next to us. What a surprise! I remembered Blanche from Brownie Scouts. Her mother had been our leader and her older sister "Scrappy" and my cousin Rocky (Frances's daughter) had also been in the troop. At least I remembered the chubby little seven-year-old tomboy with long dark braids and a mischievous personality. The adult, 50-something Blanche was lean and tanned, with short gray hair. She told us that she'd never married and had retired after 25 years as a high school gym teacher. Since then she'd owned and operated her own garden and lawn care business.

No matter how hard I tried, I just could not see funny little Blanche in that angular, sun-bronzed face. We talked for 20 minutes about our respective families and people we'd known in the old neighborhood. She explained that she'd always admired Frances. When her father had passed away several years previously, Frances was the first one on the doorstep with flowers from her backyard garden and a homemade lemon icebox pie. Blanche, Scrappy and their and mother had scoffed every bite of the pie that night. "It was the best lemon pie we ever tasted," she said. "Frances was always such a great cook." True! Frances smiled and nodded but as soon as Blanche left, she asked, "Who was that? I don't know her." It was obvious that Blanche and her once familiar family had become a blank.

At Margie's house, we sat in the living room and Frances immediately asked for a cocktail. It annoyed her that the retirement home wouldn't allow her afternoon bourbon. Margie fixed her a weak Jack Daniels and water. She tossed it down and wanted another. Margie answered, "Sure, honey," and whispered to me,

"You know they don't let her drink at the home because she wants to drink too much."

My mind teemed with memories of the woman she'd once been. For most of my childhood, Frances was the mainstay of the family—unconditionally nurturing and supportive, and always fiercely independent. She loved working, cooking, gardening, clothes, church and music. Yes, she enjoyed a drink or two but had never overdone it. Uncle Gordon—who *did* overdo it—had a band and Frances played washtub base fiddle in it. I had many great memories of her and Uncle Gordon harmonizing to their signature song, *Anytime (you're feeling lonely...)*.

Over the years Frances had endured more than her share of troubles. Her brother was killed in WWII, Uncle Gordon committed suicide, and her closest sister (my mother) died slowly from lung cancer. But when her beloved daughter Rocky lost her battle with breast cancer in 1996, and not long afterwards Rocky's daughter, her beautiful granddaughter Britt, also died unexpectedly from cancer (leaving two small children)—it was finally too much. Frances hadn't been the same since. I was shocked and saddened by the changes I saw in her.

The only people left in Birmingham for Frances were her best friend Margie and her grandson, who she told me had never once been to visit. Margie at 82 was several years younger but still quick and healthy. California Sybil, four years younger, was still playing golf, juggling men-friends and hiking in the mountains. Ethel in Omaha, nearly ninety, was still driving and volunteering at temple. But the aunt I remembered as being one of the most involved and vibrant of women, had changed. It brought home in a terrible way what a fickle and cruel vandal aging can be.

The next day I planned to visit my brother. First I tried calling him on the telephone but he didn't answer. He never answered his phone. Nevertheless, I planned to drive to Alan's house and knock on the door. I figured, as with the phone, he probably wouldn't answer. It had been eight years since I'd seen him and during that time we'd spoken on the telephone only twice. It wasn't because of any animosity between us. In fact, I was probably closer to Alan than anyone else in the family. He chose to live a reclusive life and although many had tried, Alan eschewed all efforts at staying connected.

The Whitman's Sampler had been such a hit with Frances, I first bought a box of pecan clusters (Alan's favorite when we were kids), with the intention of leaving the box of candy and an affectionate note at his front door. As expected, his house looked deserted. The mailbox door hung open and was stuffed with old mail. I carried the mail and candy with me to the door. A weathered, fading Yellow Pages lay on the porch, looking as if it were still in the same spot it had been delivered the previous spring. I skewed up my courage and tentatively rapped at the door....and...*Alan answered*! He actually came to the door!

He looked as surprised as I was. It was as much a shock to him to find me at his door as it was for me that he had actually opened it. He looked the same as he had the last time I'd seen him. His hair was short and neatly trimmed; after cutting his own hair for thirty years he'd gotten pretty good at it. The hair was thinning in front but there was no detectable gray. He was wearing worn Levi's and an open collar sport shirt with crewneck tee. He looked completely normal and healthy.

Then another big surprise, he invited me in. The living room was exactly as it appeared the last time I'd been there eight years before, and the ten years before that. The exact same objects arranged in the same places on the coffee table and the same knick-knacks on the mantle. The same tapes and CDs were stacked by the stereo. Alan was at first quiet but finally warmed up after I told him all the family news he knew nothing about. We began to reminisce and talked at length about our mutual experiences and shared childhood. He told me in detail about a legal dispute he was involved in concerning his pension from the City of Birmingham. After a short while, all awkwardness disappeared.

Alan had been agoraphobic for many years, so much so that he avoided even going outside to the mailbox. For a while he was in therapy and on medication and it completely turned his life around. Then he quit taking the meds and reverted to the old withdrawal pattern. Many people (including myself) had attempted to help but he resisted all gestures. When I contacted various social agencies, they all told me that as long as he was functional and self-supporting, no one could force him to seek help. Surprisingly, he talked openly about his life and expressed remorse at his situation. He said he hated the way he was but it was his business and it only made him angry when others intruded. That was something I had already learned the hard way.

We visited for about three hours, recalling many events from when we were kids. He got out several old photo albums, including Daddy's from World War II, and we looked through the pages. There was a lot of catching up to do.

As the day waned, I finally took my leave of Alan and decided to drive to the old neighborhood on the other side of town. I was feeling nostalgic. But as I traveled up and down the once familiar streets, I realized that everything had changed. While most of Birmingham had progressed, West End had become, for the most part, a run-down area plagued with poverty and crime.

After the steel mills closed, the dominant industry in Birmingham became the University of Alabama Medical Center. It now sprawled over more than 80 city blocks and had become the largest employer in the city. The neighborhoods around the Medical Center and those on and over the mountain were lovely, green and manicured. But our once middle class, blue collar community, where many fathers had worked in the mills, looked nothing like it once had. The red brick house where I grew up was painted garish yellow and the windows were boarded shut. The yard was a muddy mess strewn with trash.

I was anxious to escape back to the campground in Pelham. My two days in Birmingham had taken an emotional toll. It was time to move on...in more ways than one...and I could hardly wait to get back on the road.

CHAPTER 16

ALMOST THERE

After returning my peppy red Escort to Enterprise Car Rental the next morning, I unhooked the Four Winds and pointed it north on I-65. I briefly left 65 to drive on Hwy 31 through the villages of Morris and Kimberly. What I remembered as hardscrabble mining towns had transformed into neat little middle class suburbs.

Further north on 65 was Huntsville where I passed the perimeter of Redstone Arsenal. Several big rockets were standing upright on faux launch pads and were clearly visible from the highway. A few miles beyond Huntsville I turned onto Hwy 72 and followed it to Scottsboro. Scottsboro was once infamous for a trial that took place there in the 1930's. Nine young black men were found guilty of raping two white women, based solely upon the women's flawed testimony. No medical evidence of rape could be found. All defendants but the youngest, only 12 years old at the time, were sentenced to death. The Supreme Court then overturned the convictions but an all white male jury re-convicted the men. The case became an international cause célèbre and there was no doubt that a great miscarriage of justice took place. The state of Alabama eventually freed all the men but the taint of that trial had lingered for decades upon the small town of Scottsboro. It was generally believed in Alabama that the trial in Harper Lee's classic novel *To Kill a Mockingbird* was loosely based upon the Scottsboro case.

By 2001, however, Scottsboro had become primarily known as the locale for Unclaimed Luggage. Unclaimed Luggage was a huge warehouse on the edge of town where all lost and unclaimed airline luggage ended up for sale to the public. I parked and decided to have a look. There was so much merchandise crammed along the aisles that it was a bit overwhelming. I finally gave up and returned to the RV.

That night I camped at Goose Pond Colony on the shore of Lake Guntersville. I found a spot in a grove of pine trees with a nice view of the water. The weather was mild, pine trees rustled in the breeze and ducks paddled by on the placid lake surface just outside my window. It was such a lovely place that had it been another time I would have settled in for a few days. The next morning I lingered at Goose Pond for as long as I could, then headed north and east, destination unknown. I drove through Chattanooga where I crossed the Tennessee River, then drove through Knoxville and again crossed the wide, slow moving Tennessee.

I ended the day in Jonesborough, which according to my camp directory was the oldest and one of the most historically significant towns in Tennessee. Unfortunately, I saw nothing of the town. I got in late and hooked up as it turned dark. Also, I had passed into another time zone, from Central to Eastern, and so lost an hour. I had a quick meal, read a little, wrote in my journal, and climbed into to bed.

The next morning I slept late and felt no rush to leave. Finally, I set out toward Asheville, which was not far away. I was back in the familiar and spectacular Appalachian Mountains of East Tennessee and Western North Carolina. In Asheville I stopped at an RV park just off the highway. It offered level concrete pads, laundry facilities and cable television, and that was exactly what I wanted. I stopped only 55 miles from Greenville because I wanted to give the road-begrimed Four Winds a good cleaning before getting home. I also wanted to savor one last day of solitude and "living in the moment."

My adventure was about to end but I wasn't quite ready. It had been an amazing three-plus months. In some ways it felt as if I'd been away forever; in other ways I felt as if I'd just set out. I wanted one more day to savor and reflect.

When I thought back to what I had expected of my road trip, I couldn't formulate a clear idea. I just knew that the reality had far exceeded expectations. I realized that, among other things, my way of engaging life had forever changed. I needed time to let all levels of the experience sink in and percolate before arriving at a clearer understanding. The physical experience of my travels had been amazing; the psychological and spiritual aspects even more so.

Before my journey, I'd bought into the notion that all of America had become a ubiquitous carbon copy of sameness. I had discovered that although some of that was true, mostly it wasn't. The American land and population were too vast, diverse and abundant to be homogenized. The landscape and people of the Appalachians were still very different from the landscape and people of the Rockies, and Cape Cod was nothing like San Diego. Yes, there were plenty of McDonalds, Wal-Marts and Exxon's along the way but such examples of commerce were never the full measure of a place. I had driven through great stretches of country where the sparse population would have loved the convenience of a nearby fast food restaurant or Wal-Mart. I had gone days on end seeing only immense open ranges, mesas, mountains, forests, farms and animals—wild as well as domestic. The trees and rivers and villages of New England were far different from those in the Midwest, Northwest or Deep South.

I discovered there were still huge expanses of America as unspoiled and bountiful as when the land was first settled. What a treat to have seen that for myself! Because of enlightened wildlife management, I probably saw as many animals in their natural habitat as the early explorers did. In my journal notes I kept a list of the wild animals I had seen (excluding birds) and the list came to 22. Many of these I had never seen except in pictures, on TV or in a zoo.

I also saw firsthand the encroachment of human overpopulation and the oppressive effects that can have on a place. I saw considerable changes being brought by recent large-scale immigration from other parts of the world. When I was growing up in Birmingham, I knew only one immigrant family, our next door neighbors, the Kwongs. As I traveled across America in 2001, I was struck by the numbers of people in every place I visited who had recently arrived from such diverse places as Mexico, Cuba, the Caribbean, Asia, Russia, Bosnia, Africa, South and Central America and the Middle East. The new faces and cultures were making their mark on America as surely as earlier immigrants had. I saw a very different population from that when I grew up knowing only white and black native born Americans, a Cherokee army pal of my father and one refugee family from China.

I set out to see America and I saw it. Maybe one day a trip like mine will no longer be possible. Regardless, I did it in the Millennium Year of 2001, a historic time for the United States, and my experience was unique. By telling about my journey in these pages, I can share my experience with anyone who is interested. There is something about a road trip that is quintessentially American. We love our motor vehicles and we love the open road!

I set out wanting to prove something to myself and I succeeded. I tested myself and I passed the test. I wanted to be free of responsibilities and follow no schedule, and that's what I did. The experience was restorative; it was also revelatory and perhaps even revolutionary in a deeply personal sense.

I wanted to see new things and I saw lots of new things! I wanted to meet new people and I met many! I wanted to lose myself in the act of driving.... Driving often obliterates time, allowing only the moment to exist: hands on the steering wheel, foot on the gas pedal, steady drone of the engine, and eyes on the windshield with its ever-changing panorama of passing scenery. There is something about driving that urges a traveler's attention into the moment and the place at hand. There's something about living in the moment and the place that encourages hyper-awareness as well as a sense of peace.

As Paul Theroux wrote, "I wanted to find a new self in a distant place, and new things to care about." That's what I did. Mostly, I wanted to hit the reset button to my life. Isn't travel always somehow about that? The traveler leaves what is familiar in order to see new places and new things and to have new experiences. Then she returns with a renewed sense of wonder and appreciation for what is....

Home!